Praise

Conversations wit

"Simran Singh's mastery of universal law and divine principle is evident in how she lives her life. Simran not only walks her talk; she lives a life that proves it. Her teachings and writings shared in *Conversations with the Universe* are filled with a depth of heart, wisdom, and love that can create a shift in those who access them."

Iyanla Vanzant
Spiritual Life Coach and Technician
Author of *Peace from Broken Pieces, Yesterday I Cried,* and
The Value in the Valley

"*Conversations with the Universe* reveals soulful wisdom regarding how Spirit uses a multitude of signs and symbols to continually guide us. Simran Singh translates this language very well and teaches others how to discern the wonderful language of the Divine! A wonderful book."

Colette Baron-Reid
#1 best-selling author, internationally renowned
intuitive counselor, coach, and life strategist

"Simran Singh's writings are filled with uplifting wisdom and truth. *Conversations with the Universe* . . . Listen to her; she has much to offer."

Arielle Ford
Author of *Wabi Sabi Love* and *The Soulmate Secret*

"My exploration of *Conversations with the Universe* began at an airport in Vienna on my way to Denmark. I was so engrossed from the first page that I don't remember how I got on the plane . . . As I read I felt inspired, touched and uplifted. I underlined paragraphs, impatient for the work to be published so that I could recommend it to my students."

Inna Segal
International author and healer, creator of
Visionary Intuitive Healing®, and best-selling, award-winning author of
The Secret Language of Your Body and *The Secret Language of Color Cards*

"Simran is a beautiful and dedicated teacher of spiritual wisdom. Her magazine, her writings, and her being are full of love and motivating, empowering energy. Her work resonates because she lives what she teaches, and that integration manifests outwardly. *Conversations with the Universe* has the formula to create a deeper understanding of the dialogue with the Universe while discovering how to believe and reach new levels of awareness."

Amy Zerner and Monte Farber
Authors of *The Soulmate Path*, *The Enchanted Birthday Book*
and *The Enchanted Tarot*

"As the owner of a radio network, I have long awaited a fresh, compelling, 'let's look at Life in a new way' book. It's here. Visionary, author, and catalyst for the unfolding New World, Simran Singh has brought forth a unique and lighthearted book that will have you 'getting it,' without struggling for it."

Maureen Moss
Four-time award winning author and President of The World Puja Network

"This book has powerful answers and insights. Simran Singh understands how the Universe continually speaks and *Conversations with the Universe* is a wonderful guide in understanding this language. You can no longer deny there is more going on than you have let yourself believe."

Dr. Sue Morter
International speaker, quantum field visionary,
and founder of Morter Institute for BioEnergetics

"Simran Singh writes from a place of true power, vulnerability, and honesty. Her wisdom rings out through the pages of *Conversations with the Universe* as her information is deep and empowering, while her stories are touching and inspiring. Simran shares from the heart, the higher knowledge that has made a difference in her life, thus awakening the same deep impact on all who read her words. You can trust Simran and *Conversation with the Universe* to steer you in the empowering direction of revealing your True Self."

Paul Morris Segal
Author of *Raising Angels* and co-author of
How to Get the Man You Want /
How to Get the Woman You Want

Conversations with the Universe

Conversations with the Universe

How the World Speaks to Us

Simran Singh

SelectBooks, Inc.
New York

This edition published by SelectBooks, Inc.
For information address SelectBooks, Inc., New York, New York.

First Edition

ISBN 978-1-59079-977-2

Library of Congress Cataloging-in-Publication Data

Singh, Simran
    Conversations with the universe : how the world speaks to us / Simran P. Singh. -- First Edition.
        pages cm.
    Includes bibliographical references.
    ISBN 978-1-59079-977-2 (pbk. : alk. paper)
    1. Language and languages--Philosophy. 2. Language, Universal.
    3. Sociolinguistics. I. Title.
    P107.S57 2013
    401--dc23
                                2013005105

Manufactured in the United States of America

10 9 8 7 6 5 4 3

This book is dedicated to
the essence and experience of Universal Love,
in its expansiveness and truth,
fully acknowledging and deeply appreciating
the many ways it chooses to touch every level of being.

In Love, of Love, with Love and Laughter . . .
Always and in All Ways,
Simran

Contents

Foreword by Inna Segal   xi

Introduction   xv

PART ONE

The Foundations of Universal Language   *1*

1   The Message   *3*

2   Waking Up   *9*

3   In the Asking   *23*

4   Sensing the Answers   *33*

Review of Language Play: Foundations   *54*

PART TWO

The Components of Universal Language   *57*

5   The Nouns   *59*

6   Symbols   *67*

7   Guides   *93*

8   Signs   *101*

Review of Language Play: Nouns   *118*

9   The Verbs   *121*

10   Numbers   *123*

11   Names   *127*

12   Locations   *133*

Review of Language Play: Verbs   140

13   The Adjectives   *143*

14   The Human Body   *145*

15   The Home Body   *149*

16   The Moving Body   *153*

Review of Language Play: Adjectives   155

17   The Punctuation   *157*

18   Timing   *159*

19   Thought   *165*

20   Feeling   *167*

Review of Language Play: Punctuation   169

PART THREE

The Integration of Universal Language   *171*

21   The Language   *173*

22   The Moment   *177*

23   Putting It Together   *179*

24   The Response   *183*

Review of Language Play: Integration   185

PART FOUR

The Soul of Universal Language   *187*

25   The Story   *189*

26   Analyzing   *201*

27   Defining Moments   *205*

28   Making Meaning   *209*

Review of Language Play: Creative Capacity   211

Additional Resources   *213*
Acknowledgments   *214*
About the Author   *215*

Foreword by Inna Segal

What if everything serves your evolution as a spiritual being? What if there is no such thing as good or bad? What if there is a universal intelligence that loves you unconditionally and communicates to you through signs such as numbers, messages, names, words, symbols, your body, your home, your car, and in every other conceivable way?

This is the essential message of the book you are about to delve into. *Conversations with the Universe* urges you to look deeper, ask essential life questions, find the clues that your universe is giving you, and piece together the puzzle of your life to reach a place of true wholeness and an experience of Divine Love.

As I am constantly touring around the world leading workshops, people are always asking me what I call myself—a healer, a teacher, an author, the creator of Visionary Intuitive Healing®? I always answer in a simple way, "I'm an explorer."

My life is an incredible tapestry of colors, experiences, opportunities, challenges, and discoveries, all of which contribute to growth. My intention is to listen to all the hints the universe gives me to evolve, unlock the most intimate places in my heart, love deeply, truly, and profoundly, and make a contribution to people's lives.

Part of the difference I make is through helping others to uncover their intuition and rediscover the secret language of their body and the hidden messages in their universe. Thus, when I was reading *Conversations with the Universe*, I literally felt this book was speaking to my heart, my soul, and my life. It is an adventure into who you are, why particular things are happening to you, why you are here, and where you are headed.

I received Simran's book while on an intensive tour of Europe. As I had hardly any days off, I intentionally left my computer at home, promising myself that I would use every spare moment I had to rest and nurture myself so I would be at my best when I presented my Visionary Intuitive Healing® programs. My exploration of this wonderful book began at an airport in Vienna on my way to Denmark. I was so engrossed from the first page that I don't remember how I got on the plane.

Everything I read about signs and symbols felt like they directly correlated to my life. I even wondered to myself, *how does Simran know me so well?* I have always felt guided and page after page of *Conversations with the Universe* reaffirmed my experiences. As I read, I felt inspired, touched, and uplifted. I underlined paragraphs, impatient for the work to be published so that I could recommend it to my students. I wanted them to have further resources that encouraged them to delve deeper into themselves. I couldn't wait for them to get to the section containing the following information about people who challenge them, "They are here to push you down so you strengthen the will to rise. They are here to make you doubt and feel insecure, so that you realize that there is no doubt that you are secure. People will surface that help you also see the power, strength, and beauty you cannot yet see. People are here to reflect you. However, what they think of you is of no concern. It is none of your business!" Wow. How powerful are her words.

I reread this statement several times, reflecting on how often people tell me their opinions of my teaching, my writing, and, most of all, me. I thought about the years it took to not take things so personally and how often I had to remind myself and others to use people's judgments as an opportunity to look within, find the places that their words have touched, and heal. This is why I love writing and teaching about the shadow aspects of ourselves.

Simran expands, referring to our interactions with others and the universe: "The conversation is an opportunity to explore your denied inner landscape. Bring to surface the denial that has been triggered. It is time to see more clearly."

There is so much truth in these words. We need to start embracing and loving all the aspects of ourselves. It is time to stop denying and start accepting. Only when we can love and know ourselves can we heal and make a difference in other people's lives. "You cannot see in another what does not first exist within the self. You teach what you need to learn." Even if you have heard these ideas, to read them in a book that encourages you to expand your point of view, shares real life experiences, and helps you heal, is incredibly empowering. This book gives practical tips and examples for how to do this.

When I learned Simran's personal story, I was captivated by her capacity not only to notice the signs she was given, but also to follow them and trust that they were leading her towards her life's purpose.

Simran reminds us over and over again that although life has its share of challenges, we are not abandoned to deal with them on our own. In fact, we are guided every step of the way, if only we are willing to pay attention. She highlights how in the depth of despair we can still find blessings and crack open our hearts.

As I progressed, page after page, I felt touched and honored that this incredible woman asked me to write a foreword to her powerful, transformational book. Yet I also knew that it was a sign to recognize all that I have learned, healed, and integrated into my life.

From the moment I decided to heal myself from debilitating back pain, psoriasis, digestive problems, and anxiety, I have asked myself, "What is this pain, challenge, emotion, experience here to teach me? What is the blessing in this experience?" As I discovered the answers, I healed. At times the healing happened instantly, as I was ready for a huge shift of consciousness, while at other times I needed to sift through the many layers of emotional trauma, pain, and protection I had built up, so healing took a lot longer. Yet, I always searched for a thread that connected all the pieces. No matter how challenging life got, I always sought the opportunity to evolve, grow, and progress.

I believe that the questions we ask ourselves either point us to lose energy, become small, limited, and numb or to gain energy, develop, expand our minds, and open our hearts. *Conversations with the Universe* encourages us to do the latter. We are asked to engage all our senses in our search for wholeness, including smell, taste, sight, touch, hearing, intuition, and humor. Simran reminds us of all the ways the universe is communicating with us, including through music, art, books, magazine, numbers, songs, dreams, dance, names, etc. We don't have to guess, we just need to pay attention, explore the cycle that is unfolding, find our meaning in the signs we are given, and participate in our inner work in as conscious a fashion as possible. Simran offers us fantastic tools to assist us all on this path.

Introduction

*Every person has embedded within themselves a sacred moment
when the soul says 'It's time to turn within and know you are
already home.' Each sign, symbol, and synchronicity is a ticking
of that clock . . . until the individual chooses to wake up. There is
not one thing in life that does not offer that remembrance and
gateway to truth in an intensely soulful and personal way.*
                                   —Simran Singh, 11:11 Magazine and Talk Radio

Have you ever noticed that things happen in threes? The Universe likes
things in a trinity. It is a triangle of completion, an opportunity to go
here, there, and yonder. It is a chance to delve into things like war, love,
and peace; mind, body, and spirit; past, present, and future. The number
three seems to solicit a feeling of Spirit, connection, and wholeness.

Have you ever considered that life experiences play out in cycles of
twelve years—another three if using numerology (1 + 2 = 3)? Or, did
you know that the number for healing is 9 (3 x 3)? Double-digit numbers are "Master" numbers in numerology because the spiritual power
of the number is doubled and they also have an extra influence of giving protection. The symbolic number of the Ascended Master, the spiritually enlightened being, is 33. People may often awaken at night at
3:33 a.m. as a prompt from the Universe to connect. Gurus of the Far
East have long spoken of this as a sacred time to connect. Yogi Bhajan,
world renowned Guru, would teach thousands of followers to observe
this time to meditate. Best-selling authors and teachers, such as Wayne
Dyer, Michael Beckwith, and Doreen Virtue, speak of their own intimate
encounters at sacred times that are connected to numbers. Auspicious
and sacred events linked to seeing the numbers 11 and 11:11 are experienced by millions of people all over the world. In addition, moments

of significant life choice will bring about these prompts, alerting individuals to the support of both seen and unseen realms being available. Even notable celebrities such as Ellen DeGeneres and Demi Moore tweet about this.

When delving really deeply, you might discover that everything in the universe boils down to numbers, specifically 1 and 0. The Master Number 11 is a symbolic number. 11:11 is an indication that tremendous spiritual unfolding is available for the individual seeing it. The gateway between the physical and spiritual—positive and negative, reality and illusion, the human condition and spiritual mastery—is the number 11:11. And most importantly, we, each of us, are the ones. We are all one, and we are part of The ONE.

As you move through this book, you will find things written in a certain way, utilizing a repetition or a pattern sequence. This is intuitive, as it is a series of activations and codes intended to open locks within your mind and cellular structure. It is designed to unlock embedded patterns that keep you from your true expression. Rhythm and sound are what the Universe resonates with. For that reason these series of words have a rhythmic resonance when being read. It is not something your intellect may understand but, most definitely, what your Soul Body Deva knows.

Meaning can be found in a multitude of ways, and the Universe never stops talking to you. It avails itself of every possible avenue to get your attention, especially with the things that relate to your external experience.

For instance, the body continually talks to you. It tells you exactly what you need to know about yourself. It can symbolize your feelings, withheld emotions, and powerful thoughts. In fact, so do your cars, home, and pets. Anything and everything has this ability. This communication is an ongoing conversation that literally comes together as paragraphs, being spoken directly to you about YOU. This dialogue is intended to support you in making life choices more aligned to your highest vision and deepest soul desires. Living does not have to be hard, because life leaves clues. There is a trail of breadcrumbs you can follow. I want you to understand how to be an active participant in your ongoing conversation with the Universe—in fact, in your co-creation with the Universe.

There is no doubt that you are here to attain certain experiences, learn particular lessons, and know yourself in a greater way. What you may not always realize is that you are the mess, the message, and messenger through this self-appointed assignment. The wounds you hold and the dysfunction you engage in are you, as the mess. The wisdom gained in travelling through such an experience of yourself is you, as the message. And, the individual that you transform into, by making it through to the other side, allows you to be experienced as the messenger.

You are here to reunite mind, body, and spirit by creating, experiencing, and expressing. This will always engage a beginning, middle, and end. It will often encompass a challenge that unfolds a deeper lesson. Your journey to planet Earth was intended for experiential engagement. This would require both the process of involution and that of evolution. There are parts on the inside and outside of every human being that are at war with the Self. It is the journey of victim, villain, and hero . . . the unknown, the question, the answer . . . living, being, and knowing. The greatest gift of the soul is to release fully, so that it can be all that experience offers in knowing its true expansiveness.

The journey involves predetermined obstacles within the self and in the outside world. It is through being at war, in love, and of peace, that the soul journey unfolds. The experience and integration of love, poured on every circumstance, brings the peace being sought. Love would have you discover that everything is loving and good, even those things that seem ugly, wrong, or bad. Love would show you the steps along the path. Love would never leave you or stop being your guide. But it requires you to be present and loving to the Self, so that you see, and can be seen, through the eyes of Love rather than distorted perceptions. This is the place that holds all illusion, reality, and truth. This "in-sight" occurs on a vibrational realm, the internal landscape, and manifests on the outer landscape—more and more threes!

You are in the process of waking, in each moment. The point of awakening is that moment of expansion when everything comes together and for you to finally have a sense of letting go, and then you uncover your Oneness. Expansion occurs in degrees, preparing you in each phase for when you become ready to claim your truth. Until that moment, there is distortion and disconnection. Usually there are also a number of questions. But when the moment comes, and it can happen at any time, wisdom is born and an awakening ensues.

What you may not have noticed is that you have a set of parameters in your life that are constantly serving you. This structure is "You" and "YOU WILL." These two pieces reflect in ways which will always help you shift to a higher level. Can you open to the guidance around you? Are you able? Are you willing? Are you ready?

Some years ago, I became distracted by the consistent appearance of things that seemed quite random. I saw certain numbers repeatedly. I would experience déjà vu often and began to wonder about the nature of reality. This began lifelong introspection, searching, and analytics. I have always had a deep desire to understand, make meaning of, and continually evolve through this reality. Figuring things out and solving problems also happens to be the natural curiosity that is part of my personality. In my mind, every problem has an answer, every conflict a solution, and every enigma an explanation. I am not speaking of the scientific perspective. I am fully focused on the spiritual perspective of all things. In my world, there is nothing other than the spiritual, every "thing" is spiritual in nature . . . everything.

I began thinking about the world and its seeming randomness. What if none of it was random at all? What if everything that shows up, every single thing, is a distinctly personal message to the individual(s) involved? Maybe this system of messages is interconnected, so that each person receives exactly what they need to know. But they must first attain a certain level of awareness and attention in order to comprehend it. Perhaps it is spawned by an initial soul intention. This string of messages would not only support the path toward the highest good, but also be a means of diverting the "monkey mind" and derailing obstacles that would appear within this illusion called life.

Distracting illusions created from conscious and unconscious mis-aligned intentions are tempting to follow. They are bait. Will you follow this sunken, dark road? Or will you take the "high way," which asks you to maintain a steady pace of empowering belief and soul-satisfying "magical thinking"? In this case, "magical thinking" is the reality and will pave the way of your heart's desires. Each one of us is the sorcerer, the magician, and the alchemist.

Several years ago, after multiple synchronous situations, I decided to conduct an exploration of my own life experiences and of those around me. I recorded everything that happened. I kept journals regarding who was involved, the circumstances that would precede the primary situation, and everything that followed. I particularly took notice of the details, that which seemed most inconsequential, but were actually the keys to unlocking messages. It was interesting what appeared in my world compared to that of others. I took nothing for granted and began to see connections that others could not.

I was fascinated by how broadened perspectives materialized when individuals were coached on new ways of looking at the things happening in their lives. In understanding the subtle signs and symbols showing up within each experience, my clients were able to move from a typical negative core-belief response to one of an empowered positive perspective. It was clearly evident how attitudes were able to shift, resulting in a domino effect of circumstances working to the benefit of their next step rather than to the detriment of their original state of mind. Every individual's life changed dramatically because they changed how they looked at and interacted with living in the world. Earth truly became an Earth School.

Life is your major. Earth provides the room to learn. Through various relationships within the environment, you are tested. You are a pupil, both the kind that sees and the type that learns. Every experience that touches you on a physical, mental, energetic, or emotional level is intended to be curriculum created for the integration of your predetermined lessons. This "YOU-niverse City," known as Earth, was the place you enrolled to discover your expansiveness and expression via experience. The Universe is supporting you in that intention.

Life can be viewed as a magical kingdom, where everything has a place and a purpose, especially the things which seem least significant within a particular setting. I saw that my clients were energized, excited, and empowered. I did not want to live any other way. Why would I? It was like having someone whisper life's secrets in my ear! I wanted to share this with the world so everyone could see it!

Could this be right? Is it really possible to have an ongoing, intimate conversation with the seen and unseen, animate and inanimate, soul and Universe? Were others tapping into this amazing dialogue the Universe was having with them? Did others think about and see what I saw? I quickly figured out that the people around me did not and did not even want to consider it. They were busy spewing forth judgments, "Live in the real world" "That's crazy!" "Maybe it's interesting, but c'mon!"

However, some part of me knew this was the real world. It broke past the illusions, it answered so many questions, and it allowed a more heart-based approach to life. It was a consistent and constant connection to Source Energy. It brought real happiness, peace, and true enjoyment. It allowed life to be a little less serious and it helped me understand that we really have everything all wrong and upside down. Could I possibly be imagining the whole thing? Or was everyone so used to wearing blinders that they had forgotten how to live without them? I chose to allow the time and space to see if the one question that kept entering my mind would be clearly answered, "Is the Universe trying to have a conversation with me?"

I asked for experience, confirmation, and connection. And that is what I got. As I continued, I learned to fine-tune my asking. I would wait for a response and I always received one. Over time, I was receiving more and more messages, in multiple ways. Signs and symbols were appearing everywhere and somehow I knew what they meant. Life unfolded in a beautifully flowing way. My symbols became words, my words became sentences, and sentences turned into full paragraphs.

Through my searching, self-clearing, and conscious awareness, the oncoming messages gave way to playful interaction. The Universe was sending signs and symbols all of the time and they were always lovingly placed. Without question, I realized two things about the Universe: it had a really quirky sense of humor and always conspired toward the greater good. The messages provided an opportunity to see life through new eyes, eyes which provided a more expanded, loving, and positive perspective. I discovered that the primary purpose of the dialogue was to assist in releasing the illusion, letting go of seriousness, and discovering increasing degrees of personal power. I realized that our constant mission is to be on a continuous adventure, full of life and exploration—and without limitation.

You are about to embark on an intimate spiritual journey. You will never look at life the same, nor will you ever feel the same. This book will help you lift the veils that block you, open yourself to a more expanded way of being, that will guide and support you. With this perspective, you can continue to move forward in an empowered manner, regardless of what obstacles may appear in your life.

I am so excited for you to see the world as I do. I believe in sharing open-heartedly and will always show what is real to me. In this world of illusions, discover for yourself what is going on. What appears to be real may be just an illusion. And what seems impossible is for your own discovery of the "I'm-possible." Tap into the magic and allow new experiences to be completely animated in full-blown color.

I invite you to set your beliefs aside. Go on an exploration. Be the scientist and the spiritualist, let yourself explore the treasure map of "ALL THAT IS" to know what is possible. As you discover how to connect to your signs and symbols, know that you are always loved, guided, and protected. There is ONLY good in the Universe. It can be no other way.

Each section in the book has a real life experience that illustrates how the symbols and signs appeared. In addition, you will see how they were interpreted. Don't believe me or anyone. Just anchor in what resonates as truth. Perform your own study and see how life reveals itself to you.

In learning how dialogues of signs and synchronicity show up, you will intuitively tap into your own language and understanding which expands beyond this book. I am excited to share these true stories. The names have been changed, but each scenario is as it happened.

What are you willing to believe? What are you willing to see? What will you choose to make real for yourself? You can either chalk it up to coincidence or opt to jump into the magic. At the very least, you will begin to take notice. Most importantly, you will become cognizant of the question quietly lurking in your own mind, "Is the Universe having a conversation with me?"

Swirl these ideas around in your mind. Let these concepts marinate in your spirit. Engage in the forms of 'Language Play' that are offered so that you may begin consciously having your own dialogues with the Universe. Embark on a conversation! The Universe IS talking to you, in every way possible, so that you can understand so much more about yourself and your world. Try it out, you might be surprised!

With great joy, fun, and synchronicity
In Love, of Love, with Love and Laughter,
I Am Simran

PART ONE

The Foundations of
Universal Language

1

The Message

Confusion, doubt, chaos and crisis, anger, despair, and pain are all excellent conditions for growth. These moments encourage us to look at the Self: dreams, fears, doubts, inner darkness, and Light. Within each circumstance is a message, a gift—a calling, in fact. Something taps upon the heart, asking it to open, reconnect, and come home. There is something old within, and it knows of a language we have long forgotten. But it is still there, ever present and waiting. It is a special language that, if followed, can be fully discerned over time. You must be willing to see with the eyes, but receive with the inner eye. Hear with the ears, but avail yourself of the subtle inner hearing. Most importantly, shut down the doubting mind by overriding all practical thought. Instead, fully open your senses and engage the wisdom of the heart and the gut. Hidden in these areas is your true brain, your soul's receptors. These are the language hubs of the Universe. The mind may try to process it, but the gut will understand it and the heart will integrate it. Get ready to dive in for a full and engaging sensory experience.

Life is a series of reflections, but more often than not they are reflections of the way our minds distort the Light. Despite what appears, I want you to know that the roots of the Universe are always anchored in Love. Every experience is here to renew your appreciation of that inherent goodness that is within and without. Each moment, if you allow yourself to be present, will let you see, hear, and feel a distant language that is calling you. It is beckoning, in order to guide you to greater truth. Let life assist you in interacting, laughing, and playing with all that you are, with all of YOU, throughout your human experience. Consider that everything you engage with is actually you in a different form.

Your soul creates as an expression of Divine Essence. It is always connected and communicating with that Essence. You are also that which was created. The Divine Universe constantly places symbols, signs, and dialogue in your path to support full recognition of your truth and highest expression. You need only be the receiver, answering the calls as they appear. Then lean in and connect.

Every aspect of your humanity, your desires, attachments, and manifestations, hold clues to this amazing language. The Universe speaks in ways to stretch you beyond belief systems and self-imposed restriction. It creates repetition that will make you stop for a moment and internally question, "Are you talking to me? Was that meant for me?"

Signs and symbols will appear. Are you ready to broaden your perspective and expand your mind? Your heart already knows; your body even knows the truth. The mind just has to sit back and surrender, relinquishing its need for story.

The mind wants to identify what and why. It likes to wrap explanations around things, attaching perceptions that eventually become the stories we tell ourselves for the rest of our lives and future generations. These become embedded beliefs that limit and bind us from knowing the vast truth that we are.

Can you delve fully into your senses and let go of the need to make sense of how you will handle it all? Instead, allow your sense-abilities to lead and guide you into the discovery of how life is expressing itself around you—as YOU.

There is deep conviction of higher truth and knowledge within the ever-expanding realm of life. Only truth has the ability to expand. In fact, the Universe is one amazingly beautiful thought of rapid continual creation desiring to reveal and know itself through each one of us. It uses every available one of our personal creations in order to do so. Your creations are everything from the words you speak and how you live your life to the car you drive. It is reflected in the place you work, and what is going on with your children, and your pets. It projects itself through the signs and symbols that surround you. This stretching, this expansion, is in everything that you experience, your friendships, intimate relationships, careers, and social interaction. Your language is in your experience. Are you willing to notice the details?

As the conversation weaves its voice through your history within each life circumstance, touching parts of you uniquely, it is heard as a whisper deep in the soul. Your job is to raise its volume and your own so that you bring the conversation to full life and full light. A monologue is taking place via the messages within and around you. When you take the steps to respond, a dialogue begins. It is the conversation of higher guidance. It is the Universe speaking to you. You need only to say "YES!" Allow your thought, and processes of thought, to expand infinitely and match all that you are in your possibility. The signs and symbols will always lead you in that way and your conversation will be unique to you. You will also begin to understand the conversations of others, even if they cannot.

Your "YES" was the initiation of this great dialogue, one that has spanned throughout time all too often gone unheard and unnoticed. Are you listening? Will you answer the call? Will you be on notice for the things constantly abounding within your sphere? Will you say "YES" again, and again, and . . . again?

The journey of the soul involved contracting an experience of duality. You separated from your Divine Essence and Truth so that you could enjoy the adventure back towards unity. The irony is that you can never be separate from that which you are. This is the reason the conversation is ever present. It cannot leave you because it is YOU. On each leg of the path, who you are *is* a necessary step to who you will "be coming." You are always in a state of "becoming." Are you ready to discover what that really means? There will be signposts and directions to guide your essential "beingness" back to its whole truth.

The human incarnation is neither the beginning nor end of the reawakening journey of soul consciousness. It is a schoolhouse that teaches many lessons, including the ability to be multilingual. As you venture through this track and field obstacle sphere, you can learn how to take the game in stride instead of rushing toward the finish line. It is within the details of this journey that true enjoyment, or joy, are meant to happen. Those palpable and strong but subtle magical nuances to support being in a state of joy will present themselves at every turn.

Ultimately there is one language of the soul, that of Love. However, many forms exist for you to fully know this language of love and loving. There is a specific bandwidth of messages you will begin to uncover. They will support, perplex, and enliven you. You may encounter an increased speed of change and transformation when choosing to follow the guidance provided. The guidance is also asking for your will and conscious choice in the co-creative process.

Going through transformation is more profound than what is immediately perceived. You are here to remember your true connection to the Source of all things, which ultimately *is* ALL things. In capturing the dialogue, that subtlety underlies all that appears. You have the opportunity to reunite with the world around you, finally realizing all it encompasses are simply extensions of your Self speaking to the ONE Self that exists.

You are not in need of any new information; everything is already here. It has been said before in many ways. However, you may be in need of having a light shined on parts of YOU that you are missing out on. You may need to hear it again and again, in terms appropriate to the experiences at hand, within the story of your own current soul path. You are also to experience it in the expansiveness it expresses—the expansiveness you express as.

You are not just the body, the mind, your personality, perfection and imperfection, but also the experience within and around those things. You are "experience" experiencing itself. And at some point, you may also be graced with the realization that YOU are all experiences simultaneously, even beyond your physical encasement.

See the "mess" as experience. See the messages as experience. See you as the messenger, and as the experience. Experience all that is available to you as pieces and parts of YOU . . . connecting . . . communicating . . . uniting. In doing so, you ultimately remember the truth as not being generated from the outside, but being a reflection of the inside out.

Is the Universe Really Talking to Me?

I began early in the evening. I started out on my feet, but it was not long before I found myself on my knees . . . in tears. I had been in a dark night for so long. I just wanted it to end . . . or I wanted to end. Finally the tears came. I had been strong. I had held them back. But it was their time. I sank down onto the ground and disappeared into the pain. My legs no longer supported me. I no longer had my own back—I am not sure I ever did. I either wanted to live or I wanted to die, but no more of whatever "this" was. I prayed through the tears. The only prayer I had left was, "Help me. Help me. Help me . . ." I succumbed to my breaking point and disappeared somewhere deep inside, somewhere between here, there, and nowhere.

I was still on the floor when I regained awareness, not clear of how long I had been lying there. The sun was cascading gently upon me, just me. It did not shine anywhere else in the room. The house was quiet. I was alone, not really any more alone than I had ever been, but now also physically alone. There was no one left in my life. I had been sprawled across my prayer room for hours, at least long enough for one night to become dawn . . . maybe more had gone by. I awakened to the sun rising. A thought flashed quickly through my mind, "It would be great if this were a sign that 'my dark night has a dawn and that the sun will soon shine on me.'" I quickly brushed it off, a silly contemplation. My next thought, "It sure would be nice if the Universe would send me a message. I could really use a few." I began to rise up, but not before muttering out loud, "You are welcome to talk to me anytime you would like. I am waiting . . ."

It was said out of despair, frustration, and surrender. Little did I realize that I had just given myself permission to tap into a conversation which had always been present, but which I had been completely ignoring.

2

Waking Up

Have you noticed most people need an alarm clock to wake up to the light of day? Have you ever considered the correlation between that belief and its unconscious intention toward creating alarming things within the life experience, in order to wake up to the Light of truth? Consider how many people hit the snooze button so they have to hear the alarm again and again. Multiple wake-up calls are required for them to stand in the light of a new day. How are these experiences showing up in your life?

You are here to wake up. It is one of the primary functions of Earth School curriculum. Are you going to do it on your own, or do you need to create an alarm? Even the term "emergency" clearly states what need be done: "emerge-and-see." But often that part of the path occurs long after the conversation has been initiated. Disconnection from all of life, and especially the Self, allows the struggle of the human condition. This struggle is the dance of desire and the lie of being in lack. It is the method of distraction by which we delay the awareness. However, it will eventually lead to the dialogue necessary for awareness, when you have grown tired enough of focusing completely on the struggle. Surrendering conflict will assist you in engaging in life's communication. The conversation will help you to see there is nothing wrong with the struggle, in itself. It is one's attachments within the struggle that create the blocks internally. The releasing, to any degree, initiates connection and introspection as important touchpoints of life's experience. There must be a process of involution for evolution to occur. The places where you eat, sleep, walk, and breathe hold keys to everything that supports continuous communication.

The people, images, and structures that appear are keys to who you are. You can never be without your contact lens because you will gravitate toward that which reflects you. It will be the guiding force to ultimately seeing what is present in your world. You need only be present to your self. By doing so, you become the present, or the blessing of language for others.

Whether or not you try, you are always experiencing the inner world, either through focused acknowledgement or through external projection. It is easy to get caught up in the movie magic of the human sphere. What appears outside of us is enamoring and engaging. The drama is addictive. It is real, but it is not. Life is the drug we use to keep ourselves asleep, but it is also intuitive enough to know how to wake us up—and when.

The illusion is that everything happening outside is only related to what you are watching on the outside. The reality is quite different. What is happening outside is related specifically and only to YOU. It is all instant messaging from your Universe to you, about YOU. Instead of manipulating, fixing, and controlling that which appears externally, you have the opportunity to take that external data and relay it to your internal structure which has been hidden away. Opening to your experience of Universal communication will maintain that the "real," or in this case "reel," operator is cognizant of the movie being enacted. What kind of movie are you directing? Have you written, produced, directed, and starred in a drama, horror, action, comedy, romance, or documentary today?

In becoming aware of the support signs and symbols of your life, you can shift the genre you are currently living. The storyline can be changed. Your starring role can evolve into whatever you desire it to be. Override moments where you are listening to the practical mind and may have gone off script. Take an intermission, better yet, an "inner mission." Let the story evolve. Trust in the heart and gut which guide in the direction of happily ever after. Waking up to the fact that you are "creator, director, actor, witness, stage, filmstrip, extras, and the props" is paramount to experiencing the eventual "Oneness" connection to all things. This is how to have blockbuster performances each and every time.

You cannot change any experience until you begin to ask certain questions. You do not even need to know what the questions are. You do not need to find them. Your questions will find you, if you are not in alignment with your highest good. Your experience will prompt them.

If you really do not want to listen to what your inner voice is trying to say, you may find yourself ear to the ground as experiences stomp all over you.

At first, these questions will be about life—the outer experience of life. Everything will be viewed from the perspective as if something has been done to you. You may have been taking things personally, placing assumptions, or living out of alignment in relative use of word, thought, and action. This is the initial perspective of the victim.

Victimization is a wonderful place to be! It allows internal sludge to build up to the point where it can be easily seen. Eventually the pressure will be enough that life will begin to crumble in some way. There may be experiences of pain, discomfort, ill-health, or circumstantial upset. This type of breakdown creates the perfect conditions for the heart to begin reopening. The frequency of messages will increase during these periods. Will you be awake enough to catch them?

Change and realization do not have to occur in a painful manner. Evolution can be a peaceful, loving process, but few of us have taken that route and, as a result, more often than not change does not manifest in this way. The alternate method, which is faster and less challenging, involves a disciplined, conscious, introspection and action-oriented will towards positive soul changes. The human condition is that we are not satisfied in this way. Deliberate action is not interesting enough, so chaos is created in its stead. But please know that seeming disconnection, self-created chaos, supportive symbols, signs, and messages are constantly working on our behalf.

In actuality, there are no mistakes. You cannot make a wrong choice. Every choice leads to your highest good despite that choice. There is a grand plan and your part is simply to experience life. When you take the risk of following your heart or intuitive guidance, you open the channels for synchronicity and the flow to enter. There is only good in the world, despite what appearances may reflect. All paths lead back to that greater good.

Through my own journey, I have come to see the beauty in chaos, dysfunction, and tragedy. As a result of my enhanced consciousness, the route of pain is no longer as necessary to me. In the slightest instances of challenge, pain, or emotion, I dive fully into the experience and feeling of the circumstance. I know it to be a womb space for incredible learning, growth, and transformation. These experiences are always an impetus for evolution. In addition, when welcoming change, it is easy to embrace all emotions and situations, thus allowing the flow of infinite possibility.

Will you endeavor to love the challenges you face? Can you embrace rage, sadness, pain, and fear, but also ease, joy, happiness, well-being, and courage? You are here to access the full gamut of experience, both human and spiritual. Part of the human purpose involves not only knowing, but also deeply integrating and accepting that as a part of you. Chaos supports that process. As life feels chaotic, an unraveling occurs. This is not destruction or dissolution in the negative sense. Instead it is a birthing point, releasing restrictions that keep the Self from emerging out of its latest cocoon. The constriction felt will force an opening and an emergence in order to hear the increasing sound of the soul calling. All of the mirrors of chaos and confusion will be the sweet gentle dialogue of the Universe beckoning you home.

This is not a requirement for soul or spiritual evolution, but the human part of us does tend to love drama, angst, and the ability to be our own hero. This path eventually opens the way for individuals to reach new perspectives on life. Ultimately, the soul is seeking the perspective of authenticity, which acknowledges that your life is not doing anything to you, but that it is unfolding what you need to continually allow in your greatest expansion. The soul knows that life is an expression for your good. The soul is continually awakening you to the realization that you created it all—every challenge, heartbreak, obstacle, discomfort, and hurt—along with each moment of ease, success, love, bliss, and power. The soul desires to remember itself in all things and the interconnectedness within that.

Your essence holds space for you to remember your power, take full responsibility for everything in your life, and realize that you enacted this creation upon yourself. Life will attempt to coax you out of where you are, sometimes with a string of alarms. For example, alarms may appear as issues in the areas of health, finance, relationships, or career. Anything that would cause you to go into alarm. However, alongside these happenings, an equally strong cascade of messages will be present. It is attempting to wake you up. With each alarm, the messages will tell you how to rise, move, stand, and walk through them so that you begin to learn the dance of being in the world but not of it. These situations will place stones upon the path, illustrating exactly where you need to step. The initial awakening will be stirred by a series of questions that begin to bubble up from within you . . .

- Why is this happening to me?
- What is the meaning of life?
- What does it all mean?
- When is life going to change?
- Why am I here?

The ever-growing mountain of things that fall into blame, disempowerment, and shame are the very things that will support you in understanding your personal power and ability to create. They will prompt the frustrations and inquiry.

Once the initial questions bubble up, a more conscious approach will begin to unfold, allowing for deeper revelation. Questions of this type invite an inquisitive mind. Do not be afraid to dig. Dive into the rabbit hole that you are. Self-inquiry solicits thoughts of change, even if you do not yet realize change begins with you, because you are the essence of change. You are the invitation for change. And you are the change.

There comes a point when you will make the decision that change is the only option. Pain is an incredible impetus. When life finally reaches the place where it hurts badly enough, you will no longer look to or depend on others to change or fix anything. You will accept that you have to be the one to experience your life in a different way.

From that moment on, five specific questions will support you in moving into personal responsibility, empowerment, and conscious creation of your experience. Mind you, you have been unconsciously creating your experience all this time—more than you know. Now, you can be conscious about it, and of it.

These five questions are the fast track for personal evolution. If they are applied to each experience, circumstance, and sign, there is no faster way to self-actualization. There is also no easier way to begin hearing the language of the Universe and what it is telling you about YOU. It does not require gurus, workshops, books, classes, or anything else. You are all you need—the world is your classroom.

This is a self-study program that can be done at your own pace. You never pass or fail, you simply advance when ready. Graduation is the experience of rising up to truth, opening to greater connection, and knowing who you really are through all that you have created.

Ask the questions and allow the answers to bring forth another question. The complete resolution to all of these questions comes through contemplation and self-inquiry. YOU are the answer. Be your very own soul-raising experiment.

- Where is "that" in me?
- What is it here to teach me?
- What is the gift in this experience?
- What dormant trait, talent, or experience can I now discover?
- How can I lean into and pour love onto a person or situation, right now?

Questioning the experiences of life will allow you to begin turning your attention back upon yourself. The opportunity for awareness will increase. I realized I was in a state of numbness and had to open to feeling again. You could discover you may not have been feeling anything. The heaviness is where many people remain stuck but do not acknowledge this because they have gotten so used to feeling that way. Perhaps now, you are becoming more conscious of feeling. You will begin to feel more and more deeply as you embrace the entire emotional scale. This welcoming of yourself is also a strong invitation for even more messages to come pouring in.

You have been receiving subtle messages in and around you all along. The YOU on the inside *has* been knocking, asking you to move toward the stretching stage of waking up. Until now you have been sleeping, caught up in your dream. That sleep state snared you into being outer-focused. You probably have missed most of the messages; it's easy to do. They are easy to discount. But they are on the outside because the Universe knows you are outwardly focused. The messages arise so that as you are looking on the outside, you see something that leads you back in. The goal is to realize that healing and growth always occur by going inside, but sometimes this is a process, one which is longer for some than others. The messages are flashing banners in celebration of who you really are. They appear as a reminder to shift your perspective as you return your focus back to the inside.

You probably have not been taught about the magic that exists in life. You have not known where to look or what to look for. You have been taught to trust others and not yourself. Be open. Come to your senses and let them show you the way. Trust that what you need is there. Trust that you know. Trust that you are unique enough, special enough, and valuable enough for the Universe to take the time to speak specifically to you. Wake up to all that you are and have within your possession. Go beyond fear. Go into the beyond . . .

I became aware of how strongly fear had played a role in my life. It appeared both intensely and in extreme subtlety. But, as have you, I shifted into survival. In doing so, I did not realize the fear, become better acquainted with it, or work with it in any way. In fact, I had hidden it from myself. I could not—would not—see it. I disguised it as stress and busy-ness. I did not consciously realize where I held fear and misalignment. It was nameless.

Fear can be very deceptive in its manner of approach, but it is fear all the same. However, I was conscious to what was repeatedly appearing in my life. At the time, I did not realize that my exploration with signs and symbols was a language that would also support me in alleviating the fear present in my life.

Each sign, awareness, every step on the path, and the ever-growing comfort that I was being guided surrounded and protected me. The further I ventured into this language of connection, the greater the degree of courage I attained. Synchronicity urged me to continuously step into the fear that was finally showing itself to be a deeply embedded bully. I did not listen to the fear. I had an intense longing to bring meaning to my life. I wanted proof of a connection and purpose within and for ALL things. I needed to know that the world was safe . . . that I was safe within the world.

I was propelled onto a miraculous spiritual journey. As I began to wake up, the symbols and signs called me in the direction of my highest good. Every available avenue was utilized by the Universe to speak to me. As the journey unfolded, the messages came in the exact guise of what I needed to see and hear. The messages spoke paragraphs, volumes in fact, of my life story. After many amazing experiences over the years, I can gratefully say that the Universe is a loving companion and co-creator.

As the signs and symbols became more apparent, it was not so much what I would see and hear, but what I would feel and the way I was being

prompted to direct my thoughts. My life had been one of growing disconnection. I desired to fully feel again, to know my true nature. I was
beginning to want more out of life and out of myself, to understand why
I was here, my purpose and plan in life. I set forth on a journey to know
who I really am.

I think symbolism and coincidence flirt with each one of us, a courtship between physical and spiritual. When you start to take notice, the
questions begin; research follows. Ultimately, each one of us is trying to
make sense of it all. I was seeking the meaning in and behind all things.
Living was only worth it if I could find meaning in every moment.
Meaningful purpose in my story was what was missing. It created the
perspective that something was lacking in my life.

None of this is going to be logical when you start out. It may even
seem outright crazy. The people around you are not likely to understand.
Yet, at some point you will find that it could be no other way, nor would
you want it any other way. Will you commit to waking up to what is
naturally around you? As your life begins changing for the better, those
naysayers are going to want some of your "in-sanity" because you will
have reached the path to be in sanity. The illusion is just that, the illusion. There is something very real happening here and it is YOU.

The essential first step to waking up requires trust. You must trust
that your messages will constantly come, because YOU too will show up
when needed. Trust that you have not lost your mind, that you are valuable enough to engage with the Universe. This requires trusting the Self
and the intuitive capacity that will begin to develop, despite whether or
not others in your life choose to play along. Trust your newfound spirit-
vision. Not every person reaches the level of saying YES to consciously
being spirit in human form. People might think it, but integrating it
into one's life expression is a completely different level of expansion. This
consciousness fully acknowledges, accepts, and celebrates the connection
to Self and all things as a part of that Self, the ONE GREAT SELF.

The more I trusted and said YES to what was being offered the more
YES became communication and wisdom and the greater my understanding became for the journey that developed. You require no special anointing to know YOU as Spirit, or to attain spirit-vision. It only
requires your asking, allowing, and receiving. It is the blessing. But blessings must be invited, accepted, and held. Part of the magic is trusting and

flowing within the joy of each experience, as more and more is offered. The rewards are immediate and the feelings unmistakable. The deep peace and joy felt will strengthen the trust, creating an upward spiritual and evolutionary spiral in your life.

It took me four decades to fully accept that the Universe would always be there for me. After many alarms, I came to an enormous realization that the Universe never abandons, contact is never disrupted, and communication never stops. In the moments of my life when that did happen, it was because I left. The Universe was constant. The language of the Universe was constant. The symbols were consistent. I had not been present. I created separation within myself and with the outside world.

In order to receive this vast union and unified experience with all things, I had to build a relationship with the world and with the Universe. As I got to really know the ONEness Self beyond a surface acquaintance, I began an intimate connection with the experience of universal communication. This was the connection of the One within me to the ONE that is all things. This friendship happened during several years of dark-night-of-the-soul experiences. In those moments, the expressions of the Universe seemed like the only friend I had. They were the thread of hope that urged me along. These messages kept me believing in something bigger than myself, and that it was Go(o)d.

On the other side of that, I came to acknowledge and receive the Universe as the ultimate unconditional essence of love that I Am. I had to release the ego-minded human perspective of my own unworthiness. That had been my struggle, my burden, my war badge of honor for so long. It was time to lay it down. It did not mean I could not find myself in utter humanness, it meant that a new knowing existed. There existed a deep unity to all, despite my personality desiring to create some chaos, now and then, to claim duality. My experiences of challenge, pain, and stretching created the necessary change for me to evolve a broadened vantage point. I could not only see the connectivity and intellectual understanding of Oneness, but I could also maintain loving empathy with the world. I could not only delve deeply into my emotionality but also celebrate it. I could stand in the great wisdom of the Self and still guide others, despite what was going on in my world. I could be a powerful and brave leader while also having moments that made me shake in my boots, and it was okay.

Is that your struggle? Can you look from where you are and let yourself see the greatness as well? Are you worthy enough to see your own magnificent connection to ALL that exists? Can you claim it as part of you? Can you afford to deny it any longer? Are you willing to wake up to the expansiveness that you are? Can you open yourself to the manner in which you are connected to everything in your world? Are you ready to accept that it is always working on your behalf? Can you let yourself know the powerful creative essence that flows in, as, through, and around you? Can you accept that the Universe is weaving words, sentences, and paragraphs into a language through symbols, signs, circumstances, and people appearing right in front of you all of the time?

YOU are everything; just consider it. YOU are a part of "the other" and of Greater Oneness. YOU are everything that exists around you. YOU, yes YOU. YOU are Divine Essence, as is everything else in creation. There is a special sweetness that is felt when you talk to God, Universe, Source, Oneness. It heightens when you can actually realize that the butterfly, the snake, the orphan, and the homeless person are all expressions of YOU, as expressions of Source.

You can sense a language being spoken back. Open to it. This goes beyond the mind, because it is of the "Source Mind," the 95 percent of the brain human beings do not utilize. Humans are not accessing the power of the true brain which rests between the sacral plexus and solar plexus of the gut and links to the extended ganglia of the heart. Here is something deep and absolute because it is the channel that Source Mind brings in the messages. A language spoken by the Universe with direct connection to these centers is asking you to heal. This healing will assist you in stepping back in time to the places these images reference so you can dissolve the lies associated therein. It asks that you go inside your body and feel where emotion is speaking to you. Every message will elicit a feeling in the body; ultimately that is the message's greatest purpose. They are gifts intended to help you feel into your healing journey of the soul. They are guiding you to your truth and to your expression of Truth.

When I am conscious and present, living intentionally and with purpose, recognition of the conversation is constant. It is not that I have picked up a special way of receiving it. I am simply the receiver and, ultimately, the sender. My task is to be open, to allow it, and to have fun in the playfulness of innocence and wonder that is the essence of creation. I can choose to utilize any parts in my own growth process. This is a support to quicken my path toward self-realization.

If you engage, it will do the same for you. The same knowing is true. You will hear this language deep in the heart, not just with your ears. You will understand through your intuition, not only with your mind. This is a schoolhouse of illusion, filled with shape-shifting mirrors and clouds of deception This classroom is a "degree" of knowledge that you carry to the next classroom of your choosing, whether in the human realm or beyond. In the soul review, you choose the lessons to bring forward into this experience. Why not take advantage of this physical plane with all of its clues, allowing your self to grow, heal, and evolve?

Most people's lives are ready to collapse at any moment, like a stack of playing cards. It is designed this way. We build up beliefs that are not truths for the purpose of discovering who we really are. Anyone can begin again if they allow the truth or the fall. Either place leads to the same end result. YOU have dealt your deck, which you have been playing. Your test is to move beyond the illusion to what is real. In true humor of the Universe, that which appears real is likely false. That which would seem magical, made up, and unbelievable is where reality lies, waiting to be discovered.

Knowing the purpose of illusion gives reason to respect it. It is the package or framework that we are able to logically maneuver in. Illusion allows a space for unresolved, uncomfortable experiences to be tied up in a neat and orderly manner. These loose ends that build from life experience to life experience are easily wrapped and placed upon your back to carry along, until the moment comes that they can be put down and laid to rest. There is order in the chaos, as you move along with the baggage of human experience in tow. It is allowing you to be with it and feel it at close range, although securely hidden. Within the human condition, there are many levels of truth. All of these contribute to total awareness. As you follow the various threads in life, you will find an array of perspectives stemming from the manifesting opposites that line your path. Our ultimate task is to sieve through to the purist reflection of truth in the outer landscape.

Ultimately, duality is a necessary part of this whole human adventure. Even dualism rests within the sphere of Oneness. The bridging of that duality leads to wholeness; its two parts complete the whole. You are never not in Oneness; but you need the awareness of that completely through and through to see beyond the illusion of duality.

It is in this very illusion that the seeds of truth are planted. Seek them out by exploring the pain and individual circumstances that arise. Accept pain as self-creation for the purposes of healing distortion. Allow the hand that is constantly extended from the Universe to part the veil. Trust that you are being led through the illusion of darkness within you, which is ultimately the place of Light as well. Without darkness, there would be no light. Take the lighted path, no matter how dimly lit. The outer messages and synchronicity will be the lanterns that guide your darkest hour, leading you to lightness of spirit.

Every incident has a dark and light side. Divinity and life exist within everything, including the light and dark. Consciousness resides in these as well. The experiences that manifest in life only reflect the resistance that you hold. They will carry the angst and tension necessary to trigger the very same within you. However, the symbols used within the scenario will be the guiding light of your higher soul-self. As experiences continue to unfold, people's actions and circumstances will reflect and project your internal perspectives. Unknowingly, these people are serving to teach you while they also school themselves. More importantly, they bring forward the light of conversation. You are being invited to usher in the grace of self-reflection. All of life is an invitation. All of it.

Are you engaging with your perspective, identifying with it, becoming it? Or, are you allowing it to course into one ear and out of the other, while remaining seated in the heart, communing with Spirit? In this place you come together with Spirit; you bring all parts of you to be reunited. Although the dialogue is loud and clear on the outside, there is only one conversation happening and it is always on the inside. Within the central chamber of the heart, the screen of life plays. The battle of light and dark are within you. Both of these parts are Divine but neither completely accepted by you. For that reason, circumstances of darkness may arise for you to face the darkness, ultimately to make peace with it. There will also be signposts to lead you out so you may recognize your Light, in order to allow all of its brightness to shine. In addition, experiences of joy and lightness will manifest to help you confirm the signposts being given. You may or may not be consciously aware either way until you decide to believe you are being spoken to. However, if you allow this system of messages to come through, you will realize you are never alone—and have never been. You need only ask, and the instructions will be given.

Truth is your inherent power. It is the doorway to freedom. Freedom is not an illusion but a natural state of being. It is your birthright—your home. The human condition, at its best and its worst, is the illusory creation of the soul's longing to grow. This, in itself, is the greatest illusion of all because there is no growth necessary. We are each complete beings. This epiphany is a disentanglement from the egoic trappings of fear will free you from death, distrust, limitation, and what you lack. They are all steps that will move you back towards the truth you really are. These are the gifts you will receive through the priceless investment of introspection and honesty.

Waking up is the process of being "in the moment" without the interference of the wounded perspective of past experiences or future projections. When living moment by moment, every sign, symbol, and message will be recognized. In each answer, you will discover the next question. That is how the dialogue begins. Light and truth are continually excavated "in the asking."

Be patient and gentle as layers of defense erode revealing release from patterns, behaviors, conditions, and human cycles. You will discover that what is thought of as pain and conflict is actually:

- an opportunity to heal
- an opportunity to grow.
- an opportunity to learn
- an opportunity to discern
- an opportunity to listen
- an opportunity to speak
- an opportunity to be called
- an opportunity to be called out
- an opportunity to answer that call
- and an opportunity to step more powerfully into the truth of who you are

Go beyond your current dream. You forgot you are the sleeping one attempting to wake up. Now choose to dream within your current experience as an antithetical method of awakening. Why not? What's the worst that can happen? What's the fear? The worst would be your realization of dreaming and if so, go back to sleep. Or you just might discover that your ability to dream is really birthing you to who you really are: the dreamer, the dream, the night, the day . . . everything in the dream, the witness, and the awakening. Be it all. What if you really have been asleep? Stop snoozing! Time to wake up to the dream of who you really are.

3

In the Asking

Our lives are designed beautifully. They have been created in the most unconditionally loving way, without interference or hindrance, other than that of our own choosing. But they also have the gifts of "choice" and "asking."

Choice is the mechanism of free will and maintains an ever-flowing, full and Divine experience of creation. When we "Ask," we are always given. Asking is the statement of intent from a place of humility. This is especially important in your asking for guidance and support. The Universe loves you enough not to interfere—enough to fully support you and come to your aid when you ask. But it needs to know what you want. To the degree you make the choices to support yourself, the Universe will be able to match that in conversation. Regardless of the choices you make, the Universe is always providing guidance and will provide even more so when you are "in the asking" state of being. You must be specific in your asking; recognize the feeling being sought as experience. And always keep in mind that the Universe has a sense of humor. It will give you what you want and need, but that may not look like what you are expecting or desiring to appear. If some part of you is out of alignment, you will be presented a vastly creative experience for improved clarity, healing, and inner reflection.

The purpose of life is exploration. It serves adventure, learning lessons, experiencing pleasure, and taking the internal steps home. The physical body is not who you are. Instead, it is the "spacesuit" you chose to maneuver the human experience *as* you are. The body is a garment that you wear, fully fitted with the necessary gauges and systems for the journey. The physical body can support restriction or freedom. It sends messages constantly and consistently, especially in times of constriction. It is comprised of gadgets and complexities that can enhance the life experience or hinder it. Both experiences, however, originate from love. Your spacesuit functions relative to how well you care for and utilize it—the platform in which "experience" experiences itself. This encompasses the human condition, spirit condition, and Divine communication for higher learning.

Life experiences are outer representations of what the soul desires you to know about the human self. You have entered a physical reality that is the soul's resistance to its inner light. In other words, life begins as a longing, but also a denying of that longing. You carry inherent negativity when you choose birth. Yes, you chose birth. Your creativity emerged within the desire to know the highest aspects of your truth. In this co-creation with all of Oneness, lessons, experiences, and parameters were put in place to allow the exact experience for your soul to uncover itself. Birth and the landscape of circumstance was your creativity expressing in physical form. Experience is your ongoing co-creation.

Otherwise, there is no need to have the human experience. You enter with an incredible unknown power of creation. Within this power, you create your entire worldly experience to reflect YOU to you. You could call the self's creation a mirror or reflection of your inner landscape, but in reality it is all YOU. There is only One of us here. There is ONLY ONE here.

Your "creative capacity" ("cc"—or carbon copies of your essential self) also assists in providing supportive signs and symbols. This is your "cosmic communication". Deep within your being, Soul Truth sends a beacon, like a homing device, to the Universe. The Universe immediately feels your call and answers, reflecting back the necessary messages, synchronistic manifestations, experiences, and confirmations that support you in moving towards a more solid Self direction. Feeling always matches feeling. Thoughts, even positive thinking, have no relevance unless one also considers the core feelings behind the thoughts. Feeling is the overriding force to all thought, regardless of your conviction to positive or negative thinking. You can never truly get away from your self. You cannot bury anything deep enough that it will not eventually surface somewhere in your life.

The dialogue with the Universe becomes more powerful when it is no longer denied, when who you are, what you feel, and what you see reflecting that is taken into full account. As you begin to embrace coincidence, synchronicity, and everyday miracles as your worthy and normal experience, you send out an embrace of acceptance. This signal is the YES necessary for you to continue opening and strengthening—to more deeply engage in living, being, and knowing.

Mind you, the Universe is always loving and generous. A signal will go to you, your body, brain, personality, persona, and soul informing you of having reached a point of readiness to allow more than ever before. You can surrender to what is natural and holy around you, because it IS you. You can also choose to remain in the chaos if you so choose. You always have a choice to move to higher ground.

In addition, you will see with new eyes and hear with new ears. Taste life in a new way. Experiences will have more color, becoming increasingly clear and bright. You need only say, "Yes, I am willing to see, hear, and know more. Show me. Speak to me. Reveal ME to me." The signs and symbols will become more and more frequent. Just like a child learning a new language, each day will allow for a greater degree of fluency. You will begin to see the connections within your life, a grid-like matrix that graphically lays out the complete story of you, your past, your present, your future, your generations and lineages, your patterns, behaviors, and inherent talents: your direction, path, and necessary steps. This becomes the beautiful tapestry of creative capacity. Engage in the dance of creation as you watch yourself sway all about.

You can easily become aware of signs and symbols, but it begins "in the asking." Your asking will be conscious and unconscious. Unconscious asking stems from blocked areas of thought and emotion. These are disintegrated parts of you, the non-integrated portions of your experience. It will also display as misalignment where thoughts, feelings, and actions are not congruent. Any individual can speak affirmations, but if their feelings or actions do not coincide, manifestation will erupt haphazardly. Unconscious asking will result in dysfunction, chaos, and additional opportunities to heal. Be willing to accept where you are, until you choose not to be. Embrace it. Hold it. Let yourself be with it as a small child growing and discovering. I invite you to experience yourself growing and changing into a compassionate witness that acknowledges you are a process in process.

Conscious asking will stem from deepened inquiry as to why you create what you do in your life. Be willing to recognize the repetitions and patterns. In the moment of asking, you are freeze-framing time for a series of connections to begin appearing. As you become aware of the manner in which you have created in the past, the desire to recall and integrate those obstructed areas from the past will also come into view.

Once you begin engaging with patterns in a linear, time-based fashion, be open to considering that they may be horizontal rather than vertical. Instead of occurring from past to future, behind you or in front of you, all of time is located along one horizontal line. Open yourself to the possibility of seeing time sideways, where all events you have held onto as memory exist simultaneously. Why? Because all unhealed, unresolved experiences are being relived until the moment they can be loved, forgiven, and integrated back into the self. Once these shunned parts of your experience have been lovingly accepted as part of you, they can be let go of and will dissolve back into the allness.

When symbolism and synchronicity appear, they assist to bring things that have been placed behind you, into the past, or extended in front of you, into the future, back into the presence of you. In other words, symbolism lets you take history and view it as a paragraph that is all in the now as continuous present time rather than as different chapters of your life. In actuality, there is no past or future—everything coexists simultaneously as bubbles in time because you have kept them alive with the wounds you sustained, your emotional attachment, and memory. As far as your mind is concerned, the effects of these events are still being felt on your inner and outer being as if they were still happening. This is what creates health issues, life challenges, and chaos because the energy is present in the now.

As you realize how this is occurring in your life, a desire to clarify and refine will birth within you. You have the ability to heal all related bubbles of time, in addition to the experience being lived now. Many methods of healing exist, but the ones that take experiences back into the body and Self are the ones that stick. The ones that recognize buried feeling and allow those to rise will open you to more of who you really are.

"Sideways in time" means all of life experience is concurrently taking place. It is all happening at the same time. Why is this important? As you go through your journey of healing and introspection, you will discover that many current experiences stem from unresolved pain of the "past."

However, these "past" experiences are continuously replaying. They are held in their own loop of time. Imagine bubbles floating in space that cannot evaporate or stop replaying until you have resolved the moment of attachment that has kept these situations in place. That attachment was the wound or the story you told yourself about the experience and hung onto. You have held onto a story that is unnecessary because of a feeling experienced in that moment. Not only did you anchor that energy inside, you then covered it over in a desire to not fully feel it. This is attachment not integration. Integration is allowing yourself to fully experience that emotion, to know it, to play with it, sense it, and allow it to unfold into something else. This unfolding can take you to another place of experience. The experience of being stuck, stagnant, or numb appears because you have not done so; you have lodged it, carried it, and added it to baggage that is piling up and weighing you down. There is no reason to hang onto this; it was simply an experience . . . beautiful raw energy to experience.

Healing requires full resolution of the "you" in those time spheres as well as in the sphere of your present awareness. Integration in this way resolves future occurrences of like kind because you more easily allow experience, in addition to a pattern trying to resurface. Coming to awareness in current situations provides the opportunity to revisit all like situations in your life, including the originating circumstances. It is these original experiences that created belief systems which compound like manifestations. The purpose of these bubbles of creation is specifically to help you remember the truth of who you are. In doing so, you realize that you are not the story or the clarification, but actually the clarity that you are not the story.

In choosing to consciously revisit like scenarios, you will find them still living and breathing within you. Apply the qualities of healing, love, and forgiveness within these vignettes. Use deep, elongated, concentrated breath to shift the energy and integrate a deeper level of transformation. In doing so, you heal many places within your being. In addition, you bring closure to the root cause of the spiritual condition which is the thread connecting all of the story fragments. Every episode of your life continues to be a living breathing bubble as long as "an entity"—the emotional residue of trauma, pain, hurt, or victimhood—remains attached to it. In other circumstances, you may be attaching entities of joy, happiness, pleasure, etc. At the time your soul finally chooses ascension, it will not need to even identify with these. First, you discover what you are not. Then you are to discover all that you are. Next, you are to discover that you are everything, thus leading to the knowledge that you are and have always been sacred, vast space with the ability to be all or nothing.

Right now, work with the bubbles of time that are inflicting weight and darkness on the creative impulse and the health of your physical structure. Be gentle with yourself through the process. You do not have to forcibly remember everything. Know that a deeper wisdom loves you enough to always give you what you are prepared for. The bubbles will reveal themselves in the order they need to be seen. Accept these as gifts and know you will experience breakthroughs, some large and others small, but all perfect. Let the emotions come, feel them, and allow them to pass through as you venture into various scenarios of life. This is the process of washing and cleansing. The soul is seeking its true Light while on a scenic highway of adventure.

Ultimately, you are to be detached from all emotion. Please note, detached does not mean "numbed out," avoiding, or held at a distance. Numb is "not feeling," which is the antithesis of soul growth. Detached implies experiencing and allowing something to flow through without having to hold onto it. Detached means you can be with whatever happened or with whoever it is without any charge, leaning and loving into it. It does not mean you have to physically be with or in the presence of it, just that you can be there if you wish. It is very important to feel and embody every experience. They rise up to be seen and known. You will discover in just sitting in the feelings, the emotion clears.

Oftentimes, the language of the Universe occurs in order to bring you out of a state of numbness. The Universe desires for you to feel. Without feeling, life stagnates. There can be no creation. There can be no access to joy because all dense emotion sits on top of Light emotion. The container has to be cleared of its emotional debris for the lighter emotions to rise up.

Ask yourself often, especially when experiencing the lower range of dense emotions like discomfort, disease, and pain:

- Why is my soul bringing this in front of me?
- Where inside is it trying to lead me?
- What have I forgotten?

- What is it I don't let myself see?
- Where have I put my true self?
- Where in this is the real me?

There is an overall plan for who you are. You are not fully aware of this. You are only able to be who you are—until you are not. Rest assured, you are always doing the best you can. Once you have awareness or any form of awakening, there is no going back, you will continue to constantly evolve. Always seek higher company, greater truth, and follow the heart. The Universe will use language to continually lead you in that direction.

Conscious asking solicits the wisdom from reflecting upon and healing experiences. It inspires the appropriate intention. Feeling is present because the inner work was engaged to release the moment(s) that were stuck, opening the emotional body to feeling what was suppressed. Finally, map out the action steps required to be in line with the intention and feeling. This is how powerful manifestation births and sustains. This awareness and presence is an act of grace.

The state of grace needs *you* in order to activate and express. When love and grace can be fully received in this manner, the cycle is complete. When you move closer to the Source of love and loving, something happens that cannot be experienced in any language other than feeling. The receiver becomes the giver and the receptacle becomes the Source. Plug in. In that moment, the dance of duality ends and the dance of the eternal commences, uniting as One. Infinitely more language will reflect and express this.

When asking, you do not have to believe 100 percent that anything will happen. You need only be open. Have the intent to believe, so situations may arise for you to more deeply understand. You cannot will yourself to faith, it has to build itself. When you remove the obstruction to light, faith will have formed in its place. To truly know this, you must find out who you are by going into the unknown.

It is a series of steps, stages, and opening. Be patient. Let it be personal, because so was the story to which you attached yourself. Your review must be just as intimate and personal. Each time you have a reflection tell you something about you, there will be more confidence. Enjoy the procession of events and experiences that come your way. You are in the process of becoming. In the asking, you become. But along the way, you may engage in the greatest conflict for any individual, the war between intellect and heart . . . illusion and truth.

The heart reveals, "This is truth. So be it . . . And, so it is!" The intellect charges back, "I do not understand. There must be proof. Now, even more proof! It is not logical, so I do not believe." Unless your mind discovers how to be in service to your heart, you will become a hostage to your self-created prison. When in the asking, go into the deepest chamber of the heart and you will see that it leads to many mansions with endless room for truth.

The riches of the heart will always be far greater than the perceived value of the mind. There is no greater surrender than that. In these terms, surrender equates to complete freedom and immense power for right oneness. Do not fight against harsh winds. Yield and become part of the wind, you will discover you can fly. Your "wind-fall" will be the greatest gift towards realization of your truth. The struggle will elicit the questions and clarify the answers for you to know who you really are. The deeper your questions, the more cloaks of illusion you will remove.

Ask for what you want in life and receive answers from the Universe. Remember all answers, all creation, and all manifestation stems from turning in and tuning in. Turn inward and you will see it reflect outward.

Inquire of yourself:

- Am I solving this problem with my mind or my heart?
- How do I find my way home?
- How do I open the heart?
- How do I discover and BE real Love?
- How must I be now to begin being true to me?
- How do I connect with "the truth of me" around me?

Ask of the Universe:

- Will you show me who I Am? I will you to show me who I Am.
- Will you teach me how to BE? I will you to teach me how to BE.
- Will you place in front of me symbols and signs I cannot deny, as you speak to me? I will you to place in front of me symbols and signs I cannot deny, as you speak to me.

- Will you assist me in surrendering what blocks me from hearing and seeing my truth? I will you to assist me in surrendering what blocks me from hearing and seeing my truth.
- Will you talk to me? I will you to talk to me.
- Please, with love and gratitude, make it clear.

Moments of quiet will assist you in receiving these answers. Making a clear, conscious decision to pay attention to and be present in life is the next step. Finally, developing a connection with the thought that every-thing—*every thing*—in your experience is a message. You need only keep asking. Everything presenting itself in your experience is the language of the Universe, loving, holding, teaching, and supporting your highest good. And there is only Go(o)d.

Once you have opened . . .   Once you have asked . . .

Lose your mind . . .

Allow your senses to show you the way.

Asking Symbolism to Reveal Itself to You

Let the mind become quiet. Close your eyes. Focus your mind on your heart and imagine that the breath is moving through, inhaling from the back of the body, exhaling through the front of the body at the level of the heart. Now focus your attention at the third eye point. Imagine that all language is perceived from this center of intuition. Do not try to see anything at this time. Inhale and exhale, feeling the heart center, and breathing evenly for eleven minutes. Hold any of the following intentions in mind.

In Moments of Joy

I humbly and lovingly ask that my higher soul nature bring forward expres-sions of my human nature that will lead and guide me toward greater heal-ing and clearing for the greatest reflections that I Am to embody. Lift my perspectives to a vantage point of knowing my greater truth.

In Moments of Challenge

I humbly and lovingly thank you, my highest soul-nature, for all signs, symbols, and synchronicities that may assist in seeing my current circumstance in a new way. I ask for conversation that will reveal the greater truth and direction of this experience. Make these representations so clear that I cannot deny them. Thank you, Soul and Soul Environment, for playing with me. Thank you for the blessings of this opportunity for growth and remembering.

In Moments of Receiving a Communication

I humbly thank you, Universe, for allowing me to connect with you. I see what is before me and ask that it be confirmed. Show me how to perceive you. Help me to feel and understand you. Allow me to know myself as you. I am open, ready, willing, and able to consider the Truth of Oneness with all things. Help me not only see it and interpret it, help me to integrate it. With deep gratitude and loving Oneness, I Am that I Am.

Statement of Gratitude for Unity

Thank you. I acknowledge all that I Am. Thank you for all the ways I Am appearing and expressing. Thank you for revealing the experience of Love that I Am. Thank you for the All that I am in experience and expression. Thank you. I Am Love. I am Truth. I Am Loved. I Am Lover. I Am Beloved. I Am that I Am. I remember why I came. Thank you. Yes. Thank you.

4

Sensing the Answers

It is easy to take the human senses for granted. You are born with these experiential abilities and probably take no real notice of them, unless they become threatened in some way, or you hear of another's loss. Neither do you know or engage the full expanse and many dimensions they lead to. But you can.

You can open to many new experiences within this world by embracing your senses and releasing your sensibilities. The senses are your matrix feedback monitors. They assist you in physical reality but also in the intuitive nature of *reality*, that which is really going on beneath the surface of the practical mind. In order to touch this "real" world, you must expand the senses from the limited use you now engage.

Each sense is not merely here to be a way to take in the world around you, but to dance between the worlds. They provide an opportunity to delve deeply into experience, significantly beyond the mind, ego, personality, identity, or image that is portrayed. You are here to step in and out of various dimensions of experience by building muscles for these senses to partake in both the outer and the inner world. These senses are given to fully embody spiritual and physical experience. Your body is simply the vehicle for them to express. Are you limiting them? Are you expanding them? Are you in the senses? Do you allow yourself to become the experience of the senses or are you a body with senses? There is a distinct difference: one lives by perceiving from the outside; one is fully engaged within.

In looking at life, gauge how you have held back. If the senses are not fully activated, you will not be. The five senses and two subtler senses are the seven great building blocks of the spiritual human being and are an extension of the five elements that make up all things. As manipulations of energy, the entire Universe and everything in it is composed of seven elements: earth, air, ether, water, fire, time, and light. A human is the assemblage of the seven predominant elements plus the "immaterial self." These elements express through the senses and are related to specific organs so that experience integrates fully. When engaging with Universal dialogue, the senses will deepen your connection and understanding.

You are one with everything. You are connected with all that is. You are composed of the seven elements that are creation. For your benefit, they transcend from their original form into the seven human senses: sight, hearing, touch, smell, taste, intuition, and humor. They have been given not to define or explain your experience, but to gain a higher sense of purpose and create subtle components for a broadened and connecting experience of Oneness.

There is a delicate balance of expansion regarding these stimuli receivers, of which you have relied upon a mere fraction, for their sensory input. It requires the experience of being human and the essence of your spirit, from a perspective of the soul's desire to know connection within and between all things. The senses place you in the space between, a rich place of deep silence where nothing requires words or being named. Only the senses can take you there.

Viewing the senses as experiential entities in their own right will take them beyond mere tools of human life, allowing you full scope and access to the greater dimensions life has to offer. For now, just be willing to experience them to a greater degree than you ever have before. Your "YES" will invite additional experiences as you allow yourself to open to full sensory perception.

THE MULTI-SENSORY HUMAN ELEMENTS & SENSE-ABILITIES

Element	Sense	*Physical	Energy Center	Universe Role
Time	Humor	Liver – Gut – Allowing	Crown Chakra	Infinity
Light	Intuition	Heart – Heart – Feeling	Third Eye Chakra	Illumination
Ether	Hearing	Ear – Mouth – Speech	Throat Chakra	Space

Air	Touch	Skin – Hand – Holding	Heart Chakra	Movement
Fire	Sight	Eyes – Feet – Walking	Solar Plexus	Energy
Water	Taste	Tongue – Genitals – Creation	Sacral Chakra	Attraction
Earth	Smell	Nose – Anus - Excretion	Root Chakra	Solidity

Physical: Sense Organ Intake – Action Area – Outward Expression

SENSE OF SMELL

| Earth | Smell | Nose – Anus - Excretion | Root Chakra | Solidity |

The sense of smell is one of the least used and underrated of the senses. You unconsciously use it, but what if you allowed yourself to rise within it? Originally used for tracking and hunting, society has technologically advanced to the stage where it is hardly consciously accessed because of so many distractions. However, we each not only have our own unique sense of smell, but also a unique smell. Each layer of you has a scent. Even the auric field gives off a scent.

For those who delve deeply into their "sense-abilities," smell determines a lot about an individual from the physical all the way through to astral levels. Just as the physical smell denotes degrees of health, the astral level of you has a distinct smell providing insight to your overall spiritual health.

Earth represents a solid state of matter and is the element within you known as smell. Earth is compact, stable, rigid, hard, and dense in quality. Bones, teeth, muscle, and fat are all derived from this earth element. The nose is the earth related organ that takes in smell. Deeply inhale everything for a greater knowledge of its reflection. Smell is for you to deeply root and ground within the scents that abound so that you can track your Self.

Smell gives the ability to connect you to, and ground you in, the moment. It allows you to dive within the odor and become part of it, entering the experience from a completely different perspective. Smells will whelm and overwhelm. You are to enjoy them, deeply immersing yourself in a way that allows you to disappear into them. Smells allow you to experience Oneness quickly, letting you know the object, whether it is a circumstance, an experience, another person or some other physicality. As it is heightened, you will also be able to smell the energy when it changes in a room. You will be able to sense the smell of different dimensions or times and spaces, for example when a wound is triggered and the time that takes you back to. It also stimulates and enhances the other senses.

The action of smell is related to the anus, in the root chakra energy center of the body. This is the area for excretion, grounding, rooting, and releasing back into the earth. Excretion provides you the ability of release whether in the physical form or energetically. You hold toxicity in physical forms as well as emotional, auric, and mental forms which would be energetic toxicity. The earth can take what you let go of. It will revitalize and nurture you, regenerating new life and renewing spirit. The root provides stability for the body and the mind. Through excretion, it clears space for newness to enter and be breathed up, allowing the power of the Great Mother to anchor the passionate reflections that move up from her core. You too have these roots that extend down into this hot, rich center of maternal wisdom. The center is also asking you to sit in the experiences and fully engage in them so that they are taken in and then released. You are asked to root into any distortion or separation that may exist in the spaces that arise.

Knowing and anchoring within the roots that energetically extend down from your feet to the molten core center of the earth will support your stance in the world. You have this self-grounding mechanism built in. So many people live outside or above their bodies, do you? Smells will bring you back, settle your spirit, and awaken you. This is the reason scent is used when someone passes out. The nose is extremely sensitive to the awakening process. Smells are of significant importance when it comes to your matrix language. They will consist of three types:

Smells of Nostalgia – The Past

Smells of nostalgia allow you access to the past, to the memories that have touched you in some way, either good or bad. They may be beautiful aromatic scents or uncomfortable unpleasant smells. When these arise, they are symbols and signs to go back, in that moment, to the memory that is rising up. This process, of course, has nothing to do with the story but more importantly the feeling, the place in the body where energy is locked, and awareness of the charge that exists. Something is asking for your attention and it is related to the very conflict, experience, decision, or interaction that is taking place at that time. You are being given an opportunity to register an emotion and discern wise actions to use as knowledge within something you currently face.

Anna's Story

Anna had been in conflict with a distant cousin for several years. They decided to meet with the intent to resolve the longstanding issues. They chose to meet on neutral ground, selecting a local park. As she sat on the park bench waiting, she smelled warm apple pie. It was strong enough to become cognizant of, although she was not sure where it was coming from. Having worked with me for a long period, Anna had learned to embrace all things that appeared as communication, appearing to her as aspects of herself. She knew the scent was relative to what was about to happen and embraced the communication rising for attention.

A thought crosses her mind, "I love apple pie. Grammy used to make the best." Rather than dismissing her thought, Anna closed her eyes and breathed herself back to a time sitting with grandma, eating pie. It brought up secure, loving, and warm feelings. They would have long talks about life. Anna's grandma would speak of life struggles and how she overcame them. The message was always, "Serve in love and more love will appear." There was calm in those moments. Her words consistently felt like truth. Anna contemplated the message that arose, along with the expansive warmth that rose. She knew this was being asked of her. She was being reminded of the feeling of loving and being loved, the experience of listening and connecting. Her perspective completely changed from having to state her side to being open to listening and holding a space of love and warmth.

This subtle scent was asking Anna to apply love and presence to the conflict. She was being given the message of how to handle things. Knowing it was truth because of how the imagery felt in her body, Anna shifted. She opened and extended warmth and love. The situation transformed with use of the guidance and the relationship healed. Although the cousin was a recipient of the healing, the blessing occurred from within Anna, strong enough to rise up and overflow, soaking the space with what was necessary to bless the other as well. The other being, in reality, was simply another aspect of Anna appearing in her experience in order to grow.

Smells of Change—The Present

Smells of change will feel as if the air has changed. It can be as subtle as walking in and out of a room and noticing the air smells different because the energy of the room has shifted. It may also be what most would consider a random everyday happening that would not seem to have any significance at all. But everything has a purpose, small or large. If it is all Divine Essence, it can only be purposeful possibility and experience that is unfolding, integrating, connecting, refining, and unifying all things. These smells foretell of life transformation happening.

Scents are a reminder to initiate a change that is necessary: pouring of cement, wood burning, fire, changing seasons, odors of paint, and so forth; anything demolition, construction, or building related. This can be in terms of physical structures or in regard to building, mergers, or dissolution of relationships, partnerships, businesses; these all have a smell that is excreted.

When scents of change arise, they will often be reminiscent of a past choice. They will smell the same. We have a tendency to believe that signals and signs will initiate memories of only pain, but they could be of either pain or pleasure. The object of any scent is to assist you in tapping into any feeling you carry within you. This encompasses the full spectrum of fear to love. These reminders will be confirmation that it is time to move, shift, grow, and/or go—both literally and emotionally.

Reba's Story

Reba sat in the coffee shop, sipping her last bit of tea. There was so much to complete by late afternoon. Everything was piling up around her and the pressure was becoming unbearable. She found herself working all of the time. Life was not as fulfilling as it once had been. Her husband,

Scott, was busy all the time as well. They were ships passing between schedules, stopping just long enough to share a meal once a day. Reba paid the check. This was not how she had envisioned her marriage . . . her life.

As she stepped out of the café, she smelled something in the air. It was dusty and musty, making her cough. The smell was suffocating and she could not breathe. Her chest felt tight and weighted down, as if someone were sitting on it.

The city was redoing the road, breaking up concrete, and pouring new cement. It was a smell that made her want to leave quickly; her adrenaline was pumping. All of a sudden an urge to move came from deep within. She just knew it was time for a new job, a different relationship, and a bigger city. It was time to bust up the concrete in her life and pour a new foundation. She could sense it was time to take a new road. She was smelling the feeling of suffocation. But it reminded her of something else. She reached her vehicle and sat still inside. Images began coming to her as she let herself become the smell she originally wanted to run from.

Reba went back to when she was a child of nine. There was uneasiness in her body. She could feel it in her core as a dull throb extending from her stomach. Her mother was moving around the house quickly, packing up their belongings. Reba remembered the anger and powerlessness she felt then. At the time, she was afraid, as if her life was being ripped from beneath her. She could not understand why and how her mother had so abruptly made the decision for them to leave.

Reba allowed those feelings to rise and held them lovingly. Trying to quiet her thoughts, she looked at the situation objectively for the first time. She understood her mother for the first time, seeing the experience from this new-found perspective.

At the time, they lived on a dirt road on the edge of the town. A highway was being constructed, not very far from their home. Similarly, there was lots of dust and the smell of concrete permeated the air. At the time, she thought her mother was running away. But this was the smell of breaking free. She remembered her mom making the choice to begin a new life, even with two girls in tow. No one understood. Her life appeared very comfortable and steady. To everyone else, the choice appeared to be insanity, a midlife crisis, a breakdown.

At the time, her mother only said, "Sometimes when things feel old and dusty, you begin to recognize that you feel old and dusty, too. When that happens, something has to change and right now, that would be me." They moved to a new place, several states away, where they knew no one. Her mother was very happy after that. She had less money, a smaller house, less help . . . but something birthed within her and she participated more in life.

Finally understanding, Reba felt great love for her mother. "I understand now, Mom. You did it to break free from yourself. You did it for you. You did it to show us. You had to pave a new path. And now, I too can break free to be me. I shall pave a new path now."

The remembering gave Reba the integration needed, in addition to allowing courage to well up within her. There is always good. Every circumstance, experience, and situation always serves. Everything serves higher good.

Smells of Awakening—The Future Self Now

Some smells will whisk you into experiences and places you have never been. They will tantalize and arouse you, bringing forth parts of you that have long been dormant. They will invite you to have more, be more, live bigger, and allow expansiveness. These are the smells that broaden you. They can range from people to culture to environment, encompassing cuisine to adventure. These are the aromas and scents that bring forward the deep knowing that there is much more to life, and to the expression life desires to bring as and through you. They invite you to explore, uncover, and discover who you really are. Awakening smells will bring forth intense emotion and the conscious desire to change. Oftentimes, these dominate during the heaviest times, particularly the dark nights. In those moments when an individual is numb and deadened, these will bring a person to the edge, beckoning them back into life.

In many cases these smells will be of nature, new places, spices, foods, and cultures. It will be the smells that are foreign to your understanding so that you stretch beyond who you are or who you have become stuck in.

Calvin's Story

Calvin walked through the home toward the backyard. His life seemed empty now. His wife had died after a long illness and the pain had been tremendous. The home had been on the market since her death. At the time, it felt as if he, too, had died. He had not wanted to face the grief, so he moved closer to town. But the home finally had a contract and it was closing that afternoon. He had to go back one last time. His memories now were only of the last years of illness and finally days of hospice. The house felt like death to him.

It had been two years since he had been to the property. As he walked from room to room of the home, he could only see the gray. He felt nothing. It was as quiet as those last months had been. Walking through rather quickly, he wanted to get back outside. Calvin unlocked one of the rear doors to the patio. The yard was the same, just overgrown. He slid open the glass door and the scent of rosemary wafted past.

Becca had loved fresh rosemary. She would always prepare "Italian night" at home on Fridays. Every dish was one of his mother's recipes, always heavily laden with rosemary. Becca had planted rosemary bushes in their yard when his mother died and began the Friday night tradition. She had said, "This is in honor of your mom, and to let you know that love and memories never die." But Becca had died as well. It rocked him to his core. He closed his eyes, not able to deny the fragrance. It was so immense he surrendered and the tears finally began flowing.

Calvin buried his face in the rosemary bush, allowing his tears to rain down. The healing was beginning. The past two years all he knew was death. The smell that had permeated his memory was illness and decay. This moment brought forth the remembrance of Becca alive and well; it allowed life to rise back up from within him. The rosemary smelled of life; it awakened the memories. It awakened him. He could finally feel the grief, so he could live again, and in doing so accept Becca's living, healthy memory. Spiritually, rosemary symbolizes protection, healing, and everlasting love. Intuitively his mother knew to make this a strong part of her life for those around her to heal. Becca also tapped into this intuitively. However in reality, it was both souls connecting and knowing the big picture and what would be needed down the road. In reality it was these two souls, also as Calvin's essence, knowing the needs of the experience, named Calvin, for evolution to continue.

SENSE OF TASTE

Water	Taste	Tongue – Genitals – Creation	Sacral Chakra	Attraction

The sense of taste is a barometer for what is good for you and what is not. Your body knows its truth and will tell you what it is you should be ingesting. Taste combines the attributes of smell and touch so that a more intimate approach to life can take place. This intimation can also serve as a defense system, keeping you secure and knowledgeable as to how deeply you are to engage.

Taste is connected to the element of water, which characterizes change as represented by the liquid state. Water is necessary for your survival. Your water element appears in the body as blood and lymph regulating all systems, carrying information, transporting waste, and bringing disease fighters. This is the force of cohesion and the substance of change and attraction as it allows the flow of life to continue.

The tongue is the primary sense organ of taste and functions as a preceptor. You taste through the tongue, whether it be food, experience, or life. It is the explorer, open to take in experience. The related organ of action is the genitalia. It is located in the area of the sacral chakra, the womb of creativity. This is the birthing place of all ideas and creations. Both the tongue and the genitalia cannot survive without the element of water. Water supports creation in flowing forth. It carries the unfolding desire along until fulfillment and satiation. Both open the senses to the varied dimensions of experience with something. They enliven, awaken, and stimulate pleasure which activates creative action and engagement.

The sacral is related to relationships between people, objects, and life. It is the creativity center. In allowing the taste of new experiences and activating them in the womb of creation, you also activate "attraction" from the Universe. Attraction of like kind and mind are procreative to the process of soulful integration. The sense of taste is an invitation to savor all experiences that enter your sphere. This goes far beyond acquaintance. Taste asks for intimacy. Allow every moment to roll around on your tongue to the point where you feel like you have fully experienced yourself with it. Likewise, sit in every experience fully tasting it, making love to it, and intimately discovering it.

The sense of taste elicits action. It is a guiding force that helps you see what is missing and where you need to go on the path to fulfill that need. It is for the purpose of creating what is missing in the experience and will also directly define that aspect of you. Notice the tastes you crave, those that repel you, and even those that bring forth another sensation of thought. The tastes you crave are the creations that you can open to in life.

SENSE OF SIGHT

Fire	Sight	Eyes – Feet – Walking	Solar Plexus	Energy

The physical sense of sight allows us to glean tremendous enjoyment and satisfaction from the outer world. The cultivation of appreciation and gratitude for what is being seen opens channels for greater vision, creativity, and manifestation. Seeing utilizes the healing effects of color and universal language if one engages in receiving fully what they are seeing.

Outer sight can broaden by seeing things in a deeper way. Seeing must dance with inner vision to become insight. Sight is grounded in the element of fire, which burns through you as a radiant quality. There is heat and energy in the body, which is a transformational force. It radiates from the core, the Solar Plexus. It is the center of many powerful suns, connecting you to the great sun. This center houses your personal power and will.

Sight pertains to vision, both near and present, far-reaching and expansive. Fire also relates to vision because of heat, light, and color. This vision is connected to the feet, which move you in the direction of your aspirations, dreams, goals, and visions. The feet walk in the direction where vision is held, always forward. You are energy. Everything you create is energy. All that is created is energy. You are that transmutable flame which is activated when you anchor sight and vision within the solar plexus area. This still, focused presence within the core burns away the obstacles that stand in the way when you see and respond to guidance. It is the raging heat of passion and aliveness that brings forth ideas, connections, and steps along the path in service to a broader vision.

Initially, sight will be your greatest ally in becoming aware of the messages that are around you. Your eyes will naturally draw you toward what you need to see, as part of their function. You need only be present and aware. Since sight is related to the feet and the power center, your part of the co-creative process will be walking into promptings with power. Give energy to what you feel led to. As you build recognition of the messages in the outer world and bring them back inside for integration, you will gain deeper and deeper insight into what these messages are revealing for you. Your internal sight will begin to perceive distinctions within this soulful language. Although you will see one thing in three-dimensional reality, you will know the fullness of that sighting in a fifth dimensional experience.

Sight has the potential to create a physical counterpart to what is in the imagination. Visualization is a creative force. You may assume it is merely imagination, but your focus has the ability to birth something into possibility. Your continued focus, feeling, and action will bring it into full form. When the mind creates a clear image, and the proper stimuli, alignment, and allowances are in place, it can manifest on the physical plane. Fan the flames that are embers within the "sou-lar" plexus. Breathe life into them. You are a birthing energy, a force of creation and a creative source. Within you lay the fire of creation, the eye of creation, and the footprint of manifestation. Place out into the world more of you.

SENSE OF TOUCH

| Air | Touch | Skin – Hand – Holding | Heart Chakra | Movement |

The sense of touch is the most intimate form of cellular communication that can be exchanged. When you touch another, you are allowing yourself to be touched as well. The act of touching is the act of knowing. The skin, the largest organ of the body, is a derivative of the element air. Air relates to the sense of touch, allowing the space and movement for being. It is sensitive to things both physically and energetically. The hand is how we reach out to discover. However, the sense of touch can be expressed in many ways. It deepens in understanding as you deepen in your expression and experience of it. We consider it a boundary to define us, but it is the surface that actually allows us to connect with the subtler realms. It is not separate from all else. It is the bridge between everything.

Part of your reason for entering the human experience is to know these various senses. They are part of your path to remembering. At the point of separation from Divine Essence, also known as the complete ONEness existence of all things, there is a disconnection from conscious telepathic and empathic training. Touch is the greatest communication of spirit and consciousness and gets transmitted as energy whether there is the physical sensation of touch or not. You are always "in touch." The breath is the interweaving of touch and air. Breathing is the spiritual path to full integration of all levels, when performed consciously and as a technology. Breath allows the intercourse of seen and unseen that is Oneness.

Pleasure is the divine right of every being. Touch is the sense that helps you access this feeling on an ongoing basis. Pleasure initiates higher frequency. In allowing touch to integrate the feelings of pleasure, joy, ecstasy, and love, you continually imprint it within the consciousness. This supports a foundation for creating pleasure in life experiences. Denying touch, pleasure, or connection will create experiences of disconnection, loneliness, isolation, and longing. It will also result in a craving for those experiences. The willingness to have and hold what appears in experience, whether labeled good or bad, determines the degree to which the messages you receive will be supportive.

These messages will always appear; you block yourself from the full awareness of them due to your own barriers. Not touching or letting the message touch you keeps it from coming into the body to be recognized for what it is and where it really is residing within you. Be aware of the energy you are exuding. Be in "touch" with who you are and your energy, first and foremost. Then touch and be touched in every moment by what is playing out around you.

The heart chakra is very important in this regard. Here is the seat of your loving essence. In seeing the loving essence within you, it will become apparent in everything else. You will touch everything with that energy of open heartedness. All things, both animate and inanimate, are comprised of energy. The heart has an infinite capacity of love and compassion. It innately knows it is One with all. You simply have to awaken to your heart essence. You need only to rise in love. Everything that exists is the individuation of the ONE all-encompassing energy. Through touch, you reconnect to the part of you in everything. Go beyond surface touch and allow everything in your life to deeply touch you.

SENSE OF HEARING

Ether	Hearing	Ear – Mouth – Speech	Throat Chakra	Space

Hearing and listening are both external and internal processes. When combined, they are the appropriate sounding board for your choices and decisions. When one listens fully, any and all things are possible.

Ether, the originating element of hearing, is the space where everything happens. Ether is composed of all matter and the space in which it exists. Only distances separate matter. The primary characteristic of ether is sound, representing a full spectrum of vibration. Sound enters through the ears. The throat is directly related to ether, as sound transmits most profoundly from this area of the body. The ear is the sense organ to allow hearing, while mouth and vocal cords provide sound.

The mouth is the action organ of sound. Through speech, specifically "the word," the world comes into creation. The universal role of space is to provide an infinite area for sound to vibrate and the manifestations brought forward through speech to arise.

In relation to the physical structure, ether is comprised of places where there is empty space—the tubes and channels of the body. Ether allows for sound within space and contributes to the soundings of the heart, lungs, intestines, and swallowing.

There is a great distinction between hearing and listening. Hearing allows sound to be taken in. Listening is an integration of sound within the self with an intention "to know." Speaking is the opportunity to connect what is occurring internally to what is being asking to be created externally. It takes a developed sense of hearing to discern not only what is said, but also what is not said.

As you develop greater connection to your senses, you will maximize the intelligence at each level. Maximizing hearing opens the door for inner listening to support perceptions and actions. Listening may occur not only through the ears, but also through the other six senses, expanding the nature of hearing. In this way, words become secondary, as the intent behind words appears in a clear and pronounced manner. The etheric level assists in separating truth from untruth and reality from illusion.

SENSE OF INTUITION

Light	Intuition	Heart – Heart – Feeling	Third Eye Chakra	Illumination

Intuition goes beyond the five basic senses, incorporating their internal and external experiences. This allows a connective experience of consciousness in every aspect of your environment. Intuition is also greater than the mind or anything it can fathom. It is beyond third dimensional reality, your key to multisensory access of the spiritually aware human. Its greatest points of access are heart, third eye, and gut.

Light is the element that is the basis of intuition. Becoming light and accessing light information is based on the depth of your heart connection. You gain greater vibrational resonance of the heart center's power by staying within the feeling of "being loved." When you are "in love" and in the feeling of "being loved," you are lit up from the inside out. The organ of intuition and light is the heart. The heart is the gateway between the physical and spiritual. In allowing every other sense to be accessed through the heart space, you open to a vast knowledge and wisdom inherent within you. All signs, symbols, and messages speak clearly to you so that you step on point with what is in full support of your soul's heart mission. Then you will not only feel it in your heart, you will know it in your gut and sense it from higher capacities.

The heart is the communication center between you and the cosmos. It is directly connected to the third eye and is the path of your illumination. In this sensory realm, you move beyond third dimension into the multidimensional experience of all that you are. In the place of feeling, you will recognize that you are more than the body, you are greater than the personality, and you are far beyond how you are perceived. You are, in fact, experience experiencing itself.

Feeling opens you to being with that which you are experiencing. In doing so, you connect to another aspect of yourself, gaining a new enhanced version of the wholeness that you are. You will truly know someone or something when you feel into the fullness of it, when you allow yourself to be filled by it. Open yourself to fully feeling everything. Tap into the immense well of power that is your illumination.

SENSE OF HUMOR

Time	Humor	Liver – Gut – Allowing	Crown Chakra	Infinity

Once something is known, the next step is transcendence. Humor provides the ability to go beyond the other senses. Through joy and laughter, it is possible to move beyond the seriousness and heaviness that can sometimes be perceived via the personality. As a personality you strongly identify with, you attach ideas of who and how you must be, often taking yourself and everything you engage in too seriously. Humor will stretch you beyond your reference points. You are able to release identification to the personality, culture or belief systems that you hold to so tightly, albeit maybe in brief periods in the beginning. Humor allows you to move beyond space and time so that you are unencumbered by hardship until you choose to take yourself back into that time. The infusion of humor upon the senses creates compassion, empathy, and understanding for the self and others. It lightens people up, heals and cures them. It lifts and elevates. Through the sense of humor, one is able to access the all-ness and nothingness they are. In doing so, the choice to be flowing experience instead of results-based attachment, which is constricting, is made apparent. Humor is the true soul of humanity and the truest expression of the Universe. In humor there is no separation or division, nor is there thought or identification.

It is, perhaps, humorous to consider "humor" a sense, but it is. There is no doubt that every individual experiences the Universe's sense of humor. When intentions are set, the exact opposite tends to appear. Literal translations of prayers, requests, and cosmic jokes occur to help you shift into a different creation paradigm, one that is lighter and more playful. There is only good in the Universe. Everything that happens, even what seems like a cosmic catastrophe, is in support of that good. In learning how to laugh at life, struggle and chaos have less power over you.

Laughter is the essence of joy that is the energy of creation. Creation is spontaneous, bubbling, and life force giving. It engages, is contagious, and ever growing. This is the allowance of life that accesses infinite possibility. Notice how smiles light up the world. Humor is able to process through denseness of the body, entrenched mental beliefs, and emotional blockage. It can transmute energy all the way through to the ethers, creating a projection of Light through the astral body. All senses will engage and be transcended. This is the path of allowing, moving through the body, fully accessing the crown chakra. When in states of laughter, do you feel light and free? In those moments, are there any worries or concerns? Do you feel powerful and strong—high even? Can you remain in this state?

Humor has two contexts; most are only aware of its relation to finding the "funny." In the place of humor, you are worry free, carefree, anxiety and stress free. There is no weight, burden, sickness, or distress. All is surrendered and released in this state. But in the event that one does not utilize their sense of humor in this manner, the body spacesuit is configured to release in a different way.

Humor is also defined as feces, bile, and excrement, providing an alternate form of release in a more physical sense. This is why there is direct relation to the liver. The liver is a cleansing organ. This sense organ, the liver, is where negative feelings, anger, resentment, judgment, and guilt are held. Humor is the waste and toxicity eliminated from the body when it is not used as a process of release and integration through laughter as described earlier.

The four humors—blood, yellow bile, black bile, and phlegm—are reflective of those emotions that are clogging the system. When in balance, a healthy body is illustrated. When out of balance, ill health and disease are reflected. The liver supports the elimination of these dense feelings, along with certain physical humor. When in high states of laughter, focus on the liver, breathing through that area of the body to support secretion of withheld emotion. Secondary sense organs are the spleen, kidneys, and lungs.

The gut is the action center. As you open to the more humorous side of yourself, you access the place of allowing, located deep in the gut. This is in the power center behind the feeling-brain of the sacral and solar plexus, located in this area. Humor lets down the shields and guards placed. In this openness and surrender, allowing brings forth the highest messages. Humor also requires the use of breath, and if consciously taken in, can empower the solar plexus and personal power of the individual.

You eliminate through physical humor of the body or emotional humor of the spirit. Humor is essential to life. Humor is Light.

Simran's Story

I sat looking out onto the water having not slept for days. It had been the most challenging time in my life. Everything was falling apart. How could it happen to me, of all people? I had done everything right. I had been the good Indian daughter, following traditions and customs. I had been the perfect child, groomed from age four to take over the family business. I had been the appropriate Indian wife, catering to every need. I lived my life in service to others. I was kind, never spoke ill of anyone, and did not participate in pettiness, judgment, gossip, or ill will. I gave my all to every project to the point of martyrdom. I prayed, tithed, and supported charities. How could my life be completely crumbling around me? All of a sudden, I had no family, no career, no husband, and no identity. It all completely disappeared.

Who was I? Which way was I to go? How would I get there? How did I get here? Would my life have purpose and meaning ever again, or had I truly lost everything? The phone rang. Wrong number. I looked at the clock—11:11.

There was that number again. I had seen it repeatedly the last few weeks, in fact months. But now, I was seeing it all of the time. It was crazy. Quickly dismissing the thought, I needed to go to the store before my son's school let out. There was nothing in the house for Sage to eat. I grabbed my things and proceeded to the local Publix. A huge dump truck was blocking the end of the street. The workman motioned that it would be a few minutes before he could back out of the way. I placed my head against the steering wheel. The mileage read 11011. Hmmm, another coincidence. The truck honked. He had turned around and backed up. The back of the dump truck had the numbers 1111 on the left side. Weird!

I got to Publix and checked out. "Your total is $111.11. That's kinda cool." A freckle-faced young lady popped her chewing gum as she smiled at me. I just handed her the cash and walked out. Something strange was going on . . . a little too much to be coincidence. It was almost like I was being sent a message, some sort of code. Interesting, and getting to be a bit annoying, but I had no time for these strange happenings.

I walked into the house, Sage following behind me. It was too much, too big, too quiet, too lonely . . . held too many memories. I put the groceries away, prepared a snack for Sage, and went up to the bedroom. Crawling back into bed, I placed my head under the pillows. I was doubled over in excruciating pain. It gripped me from deep within my core and would not let go. I could not move from that position.

All I could get out before easily drifting to sleep was, "Help me, God. Help me get through this." I was tired, my body was worn out, and my spirit was exhausted. I slept through the day and into the night, opening my eyes only once to see that night had come. The clock read 11:11. I realized how late it was; Sage must have eaten and gotten himself to bed.

When I finally awoke the next morning, I glanced at the digital clock on the table, anticipating what I was going to see. It was flashing 11:11. A small part of me questioned it and felt afraid. A larger part of me felt comforted. It was as if some unseen force was letting me know it was there for me. Something was happening.

Over the next few weeks, the awareness of these numbers became increasingly constant. I began wondering what they were trying to tell me. I often thought, "Are you talking to me?" In the moments I would ask, I immediately received a word in my mind: Believe, Trust, Vision. I would hear it spoken in a firm but loving tone. I soon realized the signs were always near, especially when I was in need.

A final life blow came several weeks later. I was faced with having to come to terms with tremendous betrayal from many people in my life. I distinctly remember the feeling of my heart breaking. It was completely physical in feeling. I dropped to the floor and could not breathe. It was as if someone took a sledge hammer to my chest and just kept striking. I was heaving, tears streamed from my eyes, and the pain was incredibly deep. No sound came out of my mouth, although it formed the shapes of screams as if welling up from the very essence of my soul. Something within me felt as if I had died. I lost all desire to live. I had grown weary of the human experience, but I had a young son to rear. Despite my efforts to remain the positive person I had been, the pain was too great.

I sank deeply into depression. I only left the house when I had to. The days were long and the nights were even longer. I stared blankly for hours trying to make sense of what had occurred. Every time I looked at the clock, it was either 1:11 or 11:11. I did not care. I just turned away.

Eventually, sleeplessness had turned into wanting to sleep all of the time. I remained in bed for most of the next four weeks. Every time I woke up, it was 11:11. The clock worked, I checked. It was not stuck. Even, if I went downstairs at 3:00 in the afternoon, the clock would be flashing 11:11, no matter how many times I reset it. The same happened with the DVD player. When I had to venture out, it was appearing on license plates, mailboxes, billboards, addresses; it was everywhere.

I wondered if everyone saw this. Was I losing my mind? I was seeing 11:11 eighteen to twenty times a day. By the fourth week, I turned over one more time and saw it . . . 11:11. Something happened inside of me. I became so angry. It frustrated me. I screamed out loud, "Either tell me what you want with these numbers or make them stop!"

In that moment, a series of images began flashing through my head. I saw magazine covers entitled *11:11*, a radio show, video segments. I received a complete preview of the premiere issue. I saw every page, graphic, interview, and article. I could read the words, as if they had been branded in my brain. I downloaded a sacred geometric logo and in my mind immediately knew the full meaning of each circle and the combination of all of them. In addition, there was an awareness of signs and symbols. I saw how life really worked and received the words, "Do this now! You will heal. Others will heal."

In that moment, I understood that the 11:11 had been communication all along. It was a language guiding me to know that I was being watched over, protected, and supported. It was suggesting that I listen to my heart and avoid any negative thoughts or inclinations. I was being asked to be a witness and learn this language, in its entirety of expression.

I had a feeling that I was to learn, heal, and create for my own journey at this time. But some part of me understood that I was being prepared to share information of a greater nature. If I was being spoken to in numbers and signs, I wondered how many other ways were we being spoken to. I heard an inner voice speak, "In all ways, always."

Why was I being asked? My background was fashion design and merchandising. I had no knowledge of publishing or writing. But something had awakened in me. It was a project that would take me out of my pain. It would allow for creativity and the chance to produce something beautiful and meaningful in the world. I remembered something an intuitive once told me, "Depression is a cry for creativity."

I was aware that I needed to feel again. I recognized that I needed to be able to see myself as beautiful, independent, and strong. It was necessary to find out who I could be, without needing the support or approval of anyone else. This provided an opportunity to build my confidence again. There was creativity inside of me that desired to heal me and express through me.

I went to my office on the first floor and began typing what I saw in my head. I also sent emails inquiring about interviews with people I never imagined would respond, much less agree. Over the course of the next month, I compiled all of the content that I had seen in the vision of the Premiere Issue. I was thrilled to complete the document. But once finished, I had no way to create the graphics. That would require a graphic designer. I turned my chair toward the back of the room.

A small digital clock was sitting in the corner; it was flashing 11:11. It was a sign. Somehow I knew everything was going to be fine. It was time to speak out loud again. "I have done what you asked, but I do not know any graphic designers. And I am not going out to look for one. If you really want this magazine to reach people, you will have to bring the graphic designer to me." I turned out the lights and went up to bed.

That night, a huge lightning storm came through. It knocked out power and blew some fuses. My computer crashed. Everything I worked on for the past month was gone, in an instant. I opened the phone book in search of help. My eye landed on Computer Guru. Well, I am Indian, it resonated. It made sense to call a "guru." I immediately called the computer technician and asked him to come out as soon as possible.

He spent most of the next day at my home working with the computer. After several hours, he was able to restore only one file. It was titled 11:11. As he was leaving, he asked what I was working on. I told him I had recently been inspired to create a life enhancement magazine. His next words astounded me.

"Really? I have a dear friend who is going through a tough time. She could really use some extra money right now, and she is a fabulous graphic designer.'

What I had asked for had been provided. It had been brought directly into my home like I requested. That was the moment that it landed within me. We can converse with the Universe in a tangible way. I also realized that things are not always as they appear. The storm that caused my computer crash was actually a blessing. Everything that happens is for our good, if we allow ourselves to recognize that. We are never ever alone.

I also realized that "the asking" brought forward what I needed. This was the beginning of what has continued to be a magical journey of symbols and signs, encompassing numbers and so much more.

Review of Part One: Language Play Foundations

Language Play creates an opening within to integrate your experience fully. Each section engages you in inquiry that ultimately supports learning the language of the universe. This is not work. It is play, intended to be engaged in with curiosity and adventure. You will develop the mechanics necessary to more easily have your conversation with the Universe.

Language Play Foundations support you in establishing new ground for your reality, one in which you begin to understand that nothing is random. It will support you in realizing that everything in your experience is appearing for your highest good. Ultimately, you may engage with the idea, that these things that are happening are not only here for you, but as you and the overall experience of you.

When it feels as if life is kicking you down, you may find yourself asking:

- Why is this happening to me?
- What is the meaning of life?
- What does it all mean?
- When is life going to change?
- Why am I here?

When you are ready to take charge of your life and take back your power, ask

- Where is "that" in me?
- What is it here to teach me?
- What is the gift in this experience?
- What dormant trait, talent, or experience can I now discover?
- How can I lean into and pour love onto what is happening right now?

When you have something reminiscent of an earlier emotion or experience, ask:

- Why is my soul bringing this in front of me?
- Where inside is it trying to lead me?
- What have I forgotten?
- What is it I don't remember?
- Where have I put my true self?
- Where in this is the real me?

When you have tapped into your senses and want to delve deeper, ask:

- Am I solving this problem with my mind or my heart?
- How do I find my way home?
- How do I open my heart?
- How do I discover real Love?
- How must I be now to begin being true to me?
- How do I connect with the "truth of me" around me?

Then ask of Life:

- Will you to show me who I Am?
- Will you to teach me how to BE?
- Will you to place in front of me symbols and signs I cannot deny, as you I speak to me?
- Will you to assist me in surrendering what blocks me from hearing and seeing my truth?
- Will you to talk to me—are you talking to me?
- Please, with love and gratitude, make it clear.

Asking the Universe for Answers:

Know your question. Ask the Universe to reveal guidance or messages related to the specific question. If wanting proof of something, ask for a specific item to be shown to you. Be awake and aware. Trust.

PART TWO

The Components of
Universal Language

5

The Nouns

Every language consists of certain components that support making fragments, sentences, and paragraphs. The Universe is no different in how it speaks to you. It uses nouns, verbs, adjectives, and punctuation and allows everything to be the "words" that make up the statements being spoken. The Universe uses everything in your experience to create the pieces and parts of the dialogue.

In looking at language, the most important parts of a sentence tend to be the subject, or noun, and the verb, or action. The nouns are a clear image. They are the main event to focus upon. They help to establish the atmosphere and imagery of a scenario and everything following will be in reference to that point.

In the realm of soul language, nouns are items in your external reality which will be subjective to your hidden wound or unconscious behavior. They are the tangible items that are speaking directly to how you are in the world, who you are being, and what you are presenting yourself as. They illustrate you. They are you, your mind, your thoughts, your heart, your being. They reflect to you where in consciousness you currently sit.

Your state of consciousness dictates what experiences appear in front of you, as a reflection. The specific items within the experience are the nouns, verbs, and adjectives that offer more positive guidance to resolving the real issue at hand. When experiences show up in life, they are really symptoms asking you to discover a cause. This is how your soul is leading and guiding you. It will show you where you are in consciousness, but will also give you guide posts toward who you really are. Ultimately, on some level, you do know your truth and that is why everything is always for your good. By default, your language will illustrate a path out of your obstacles, while it displays those very obstacles. It will use the things in your environment that symbolize the truth of the situation, while being disguised in the illusion of a challenge. You will always be shown images that create an emotional response or a coincidental feeling because the Universe knows you, and what touches you.

Nouns are the expression of "who you are." Obstacles, dysfunction, or chaos that displays itself is the wounded unhealed side of you. Your essence, strength, and light are the remembrance you are moving toward. In the soul language, dialogue is only presented in the combined context of present and reality. The dialogue may appear as illusion but the message behind it is very real.

The chaos is "the present" you are being given. It is, "at present," the you who you are not aware of, and it is for you to "be present" to yourself. The choice you must make is whether or not you will buy into the illusion that has appeared in front of you or open to the vast reality of truth behind its happening. That is the real truth of who you are. Will you 'present' the real YOU to the world by seeing from a perspective other than your identity?

The symbols in the chaos are to remind you to connect to what is real, what is good, that which is truthful about you. They appear to help you see a larger landscape unfolding instead of the limited perception of the human condition. Nouns will appear as signs, symbols, and guides within experience. They will help raise your emotional scale so that your vibratory frequency increases to attract more solutions. But because we have free will and choice, you will be presented things that are ambiguous, allowing you to choose how to look at them. Initially, these may be things to trigger you, causing judgment, blame, or distress. Mind you, if that happens, you are seeing and reacting from the usual patterns of your wounded self. The first step is to feel and know the unknown parts of you. The Universe knows just what to orchestrate to invite this. If you have been numb, feeling will be activated. In this case anger, blame, and shame are higher than numbness. If also choosing to see your reactions, you will begin making choices. As you become more conscious and begin to awaken, your level of reactivity will lessen. You will move into upper levels of the emotional scale. You will venture into response mode.

At this level, higher frequency emotions will reveal, inviting a different array of messages. Your ascent is towards knowing the complete presence of love. Synchronicity is the epitome of Love and the foundation of this universal language. Love is the field everything rests in and holds all of the pieces and parts playing along.

The enigma of love is that it has been turned into a verb when in actuality it is a noun. Too many think they have to do love, give love, take love, have love, make love, be loving, or show love. But that would mean that love could get tired, depleted, change, increase, decrease, or stop. This is not possible. Love just is. You are "in love" all the time. YOU are "in love" in every moment, whether conscious of it or not. Everything is in love regardless of how it sounds, what it does, or the manner it portrays. You are in love with everyone and everything all the time. When reaching the point of also considering that the very thing that has broken open an old wound, triggered you, or caused upset is Love and in love, open to what that experience is really trying to show you about YOU. These Nouns will appear as a variety of symbols, signs, and guides. They are here to provide a new perspective for you.

Genesis the Game

In the beginning was Light and sound that creatively expressed as word, will, and desire. This Source was comprised of love, sound, energy, and light. The Source was not only powerful, but also cognizant of the power it possessed. It sought to know more of itself, not from an ego stance but one of creativity and inspiration. Source desired an opportunity to rediscover its beauty, knowledge, infiniteness, and creativity. Source desired to play and, upon this platform, the world stage would begin.

As Source chose to fill the roles that came available, a great legacy began; one that would encompass the greatest story of all time in which every character would be allowed to play victim and victimizer, hero and villain, god and devil. The ultimate battle between good and evil would unfold through the word spoken by the inner voice. This duality would be the basis of a curriculum for growth, evolution, and remembrance. Source created a magnificent opportunity of discovery—self-discovery, because that is what Source willed for itself.

Within this grand game of life, many blessings would be bestowed. In fact, everything would be a blessing, regardless of its expression because all was good. The wisdom of a high council could be accessed. For those willing to know the secret chamber—consisting of the Higher Self, the Holy Self, angels, guardians, guides, Ascended Masters, animal totems, Light beings, and energetic realms—additional credits and options could be earned. The gift of intuition would be placed within each participant along with a glandular and energetic structure that allowed limitless possibilities. A channel of breath would be the life support of the cosmos as Source inhaled and exhaled creation in and of itself. In addition, there would be free will that no other, not even Source, would override, because Source actually was willing it through another form of itself.

Hidden treasure is available to every participant as they maneuver this earthly plane. Special badges of honor can be attained with skill and experience. In order to discover them, the participant would be provided challenges and obstacle courses to engage in.

A high tech response vehicle would be granted to each participant. This transportation system would transform and perform in direct correlation to the programming of the driver. Special gauges would assist in keeping it balanced and reflective of one's position in the game. When the vehicle became inoperable or incapacitated, the game for that piece would be over.

Finally, each player is given a team of other players that it goes and grows with. Through the interaction of other team members, the participant will advance or regress. A select number of team members have the ability to imprint programming into the player in the first quarter of the game. All subsequent team members are chosen by the player but will carry imprints similar to the initial team. The team in conjunction with all other teams will have the power to create the landscape that is the world. This landscape will be the training ground for learning, as well as mirroring different plays.

Every participant would plan out the details of their game prior to engaging. It would be, in a sense, a contract of who they would be, the circumstances they would function in, the obstacles that could be encountered, the team members they would interact with, and the life lessons to be earned. Free will and the power of choice would always be not only a birthright but sacred inheritance.

A Sacred Contract Revealed

Once upon a time, there existed All That Is. This Allness, which some call God or Source, revealed itself as a luminous, beautiful energy. It sparkled, glowed, and shimmered. It vibrated with celestial sound, tone, and frequency. Radiating from it was light, color, and warmth. This nebulous energy knew of its greatness, its power, and perfection. The knowing of itself was steeped in deep love and gratitude.

A moment in timelessness came where the sounds of self-acknowledgment emanated from different parts of the God cloud, sending bursts of color and light throughout itself. As the communication heightened, a small ball of God energy burst off in excitement and passion, separating from the larger mass. Before returning to its wholeness, it floated in admiration of the Allness that it was. The desire began. Will unfolded. The words came.

The Small Godburst: I am so enamored by the beauty that I AM, the greatness that I AM, the magnificence that I AM. I know myself to be All That Is! I desire to experience I AM again and again. My experience of I AMness could be grander if I knew myself as new.

The greater mass, Source, sounded harmonious frequencies in acknowledged joyful response.

Small Godburst: I hold gratitude for eternally seeing I AM presence in such magnitude, to feel this limitless possibility in every moment, to know my infinite creative essence in all ways. How expansive I AM!

Again, Source sounded with harmonious frequencies in acknowledged response. Its energy heightened and the heavens glowed in magnificent hues. Beautiful sound expressed everywhere. In that instant, the power of its glow brought forth two more Godbursts.

Second Godburst: I too wish to know, again and again, my Allness. But to know I AM as new, to rediscover the I AMness, I would have to not know.

Small Godburst: How could that be? I know I AM. How could I not know I AM? And, how would I come to know I AM again?

Third Godburst: I have it! What is it you most want to rediscover about your I AMness? What is your greatest celebration? If you could choose your discovery of I AMness, what would that look like?

Small Godburst: I would discover I AM immense power, I AM unconditional love, I AM beauty and expression. But, I already know these things.

Third Godburst: Yes, I AM. But, what if you did not? What if All-ness chose to forget? What if we set the stage for learning exactly what we desire to discover? To know these things, we would first have to experience their opposites. In experiencing the opposite, a choice would have to be made to remember or rediscover the truth I AM.

Small Godburst: But how could that be possible?

Third Godburst: I AM shall have play. Through play, I AM can support one another in achieving unique discovery. I will to be your Father. I shall be distant and hard, eventually abandoning you. At first, the abandonment would be emotional. In time it may be physical if I choose to take that path. I will have an addiction that will pull me away. You will feel ignored and unseen. When I do see you, it will be to push you too hard or to tell you that you are not accomplishing enough. I will use harsh tones or actions.

Second Godburst: Yes! And I AM to be your Mother. I too will feel ignored. I will have lost my voice and purpose because I set aside my dreams and aspirations. Because of this, I sink into depression. I will not be present for you. I'll be in the room, but I will be in some distant place. My temper will be short. Although I will love you, I will not be able to fully love you because I am unable to know love myself.

Small Godburst: I do not understand. Those plays sound challenging. Why would you have such an experience? What could be gained by such obstacles, discomfort, and pain?

Third Godburst: You have burst forth with the will to know yourself. I AM loves you enough to be the pieces and parts to help you create your story. I AM would choose to have such an experience so you may have discovery. I AM loves you enough to play these roles. I AM loves you enough to create circumstances where you may choose to be as your parental role models have illustrated, or take a different path and remember who you really are.

Second Godburst: Yes, to step into your power, you must first experience control by others or a scenario where you feel powerless. To discover unconditional love, your caregivers and intimate relations must provide you the setting of conditional love. To recognize your beauty and worth, you will see yourself as unworthy and may even encounter your own ugliness. To know health, you would take on dis-ease. To know wealth, lack and limitation must first color your experience. I AM loves you enough to let you rediscover the greater I-AM Self in all of its grandness. We too will have sacred contracts allowing for options to remember who we are.

Small Godburst: To be those people, you would have experiences that molded you in this manner. Your play would be filled with obstacles and pain. Why would you do that for me?

Second Godburst: Not only do we love you that much, we love ourselves enough to choose experiences that serve growth, remembrance, and All That Is Go(o)d.

The larger cloud of God Essence harmonized in agreement. The excitement built as will and desired magnified, allowing Go(o)d to become All That Is. In the beginning was the word. With the word came the story and I AM became separated and fragmented for the purpose of "re-membering" and coming back into "(w)hol-i-ness."

In the separation, all of creation was created as reflections of the I AM presence reflecting as mirrors all of creation that played itself out, until no more mirrors existed, only the one unified force that broke through all illusions and pain for the full reflection of itself again as pure presence in and of itself.

We are each God-bursts who have chosen roles, living specific stories and gleaning desired lessons. Other God-bursts loved you enough to participate. Those people, particularly the ones who have hurt us, are the souls that loved so deeply they were willing to be the villain in your play.

Certain lessons we all chose are forgiveness, self-love, courage, compassion, and confidence. The ultimate forgiveness is for the self for choosing painful experiences. The deepest love of self comes from cherishing the body and soul enough to allow an easy and gentle path of experiences on its way back home. Finally, we are here to acquire the confidence to not only live our Go(o)dness on Earth, but also claim that Go(o)d Beingness eternally. Earth school curriculum continues until we rightly place ourselves back in the truthful knowing of Divine power.

6

Symbols

The Universe is filled with a multitude of symbols. Each symbol is a representation of Love. It is a depiction of the connectedness between all things and the pulse that appears to say, "Here I Am. I Am that I Am." It is the Universal Essence expressing in, as, and through. It is speaking in and between all of the elements of your experience. You are the language as well. Symbols are, in Essence, YOU, and that which surges in, as, and through you. It is how Oneness continually expresses as creation. It is how "I AM" is talking to YOU as you . . . being me. There is only you and ONEness in the room. This means anyone or anything speaking to you is also YOU. Whether you can comprehend that at this moment or not, what if the entire world and everything in it were specifically and only here for you: every person, object, and situation.

Anything coming into your experience speaks to you because you have been speaking to it on some level of your experience: consciously, unconsciously, energetically, physically, soulfully. This commune has cellular recognition even if you are not consciously aware. This creates vibratory attraction and the initial visual, auditory, or sensory based connection.

Every symbol manifests in front of you as the Love you thought you left behind when you came to Earth School and lost yourself, gave yourself away, or forgot who you are. The things that do not feel good to you . . . they are you. They are the pieces of resistance you have to yourself. These are pieces and parts of you coming forward to be reclaimed and reintegrated. Creation has provided incredibly beautiful diversity in its mirroring expressions of YOU. This is how you shape-shift before you realize the power you truly have to shape-shift. Each individual is on the journey toward Self-realization. There could be no more beautiful interactive experiential laboratory than Earth School. You are the test subject, the experiment, and the scientist. Herein, you are the scientific aspect within spirituality.

The Self also exists in the beauty of the world, the things that support the celebration that you are. Self longs to find itself in the brightness of the star, the innocence of a baby, and in the flight of a butterfly. The Self desires to flow abundantly as a waterfall, strike like lightning, share itself as wind blowing through trees, and reach the high peak of the tallest mountain. How do you know these things are you? They feel good to you. They bring you happiness and joy. You can only recognize that which you are! These are not coincidences, a blur of vision, or something that needs second-guessing. Simply open your mind and consider expanding into them. Let the heart tell you what they feel like. Let these things speak into you before allowing the mind to chatter its perspective.

Recognition of any of these things may cause you to stop for a moment and quietly ponder. Something will cause you to become still, even if only for a few seconds. It will bring you to momentary presence before you are whisked back into your multitude of distractions. The deepest part of you knows you are more than you believe yourself to be. You are more than your identity, personality, mind, body, or soul. In the deep recesses of your mind, wonder is happening. Whether it is a cloud expressing as a face or image, a tree reaching towards you, a mountain sending strength, an animal bringing its gifts, the weather expressing your emotion, people acting like complete reflections, or experiences playing out your deepest behaviors . . . YES! The Universe IS talking to YOU!

People: Mirror, Mirror—The Fairest Reflections of All

The most magnificent messages come through other people. How simply ingenious that we attract that which we are. The people that trigger, annoy, get under our skin, anger, upset, and push our buttons are the best representations of what we do not want to see about ourselves. They are illustrating exactly what our inner landscape holds. On the same note, those that we love, admire, celebrate, enjoy, adore, and are inspired by show us exactly who we are. They illustrate the topography of our soul.

There really is only one of us in the room. It may appear as though you are having an individual experience, but in reality, each person is here to be the center of the Universe. This is not in an egotistical sense but from the perspective of reality creation. Every person comes in to learn the same lessons and discover the exact same truths, while discovering how to identify with others, and as others. Source appears with different faces and bodies to assist in learning lessons and garnering gifts. There is only you and God in the room, so there is really only one of us here and that is God. Can this be a possibility in your current reality? Are you willing to see the other as Divine Presence? Can you see yourself as Divine Presence? Can you see every single thing as Divine Presence? Will you argue the point? What belief holds you back? Is that belief based on love or fear? Only Love is the answer to all questions. Will you question what God is capable of? Will you say what God can and cannot do? Will you fall into Love enough to see larger than you ever have before?

What if your brother is God? Your child? A priest, rock star, or drug addict? The reflection in the mirror? Would you treat them differently? Better yet, would you experience your Self differently? Well, why do you think God created all of this? What if there is Go(o)d in everything? What if every circumstance and every situation, regardless of appearance, is happening for a greater Go(o)d to unfold?

What if bad or evil were just another self-created, self-imposed story for the purposes of lack and limitation? What if there is no bad or evil? Does the need to see bad or evil originate from a deep-seated need to see these things within yourself? Mind you, any negative beliefs would be false. Nonetheless, they are being brought to your awareness not to see the person outside of you, but to allow them to be the mirror that reflects back your innermost thoughts, feelings, and behaviors. What if everything serves?

Those that surround you are for your growth and evolution. They are here to push your buttons so that you become aware of the behaviors that triggered you, look within, and notice the same behavior. They are here to push you down so that your will to rise strengthens. They are here to make you doubt and feel insecure, so that you realize that there is no doubt that you are secure. Eventually, your inner authority must override any opinions or behaviors of others. In addition, there will be people who help you see the power, strength, and beauty you have not yet seen.

Other individuals will come forward that inspire and lift you up so that you breathe big and stand tall with their vision of you.

People are here to reflect you. However, what they think of you is of no concern. It is none of your business! It is only of value if the statements trigger and upset you. This turmoil reveals that they have said something that you believe on some level. The conversation is an opportunity to explore your denied inner landscape. Bring to surface the denial that has been triggered. It is time to see a little more clearly. If healing occurs, such statements in the future will not affect you. You will know it is projection because there is no heat, no judgment.

Others may speak to you in ways that are critical or complimentary. These statements are reflections of what you really think about yourself. There could be minor statements from, "You should not have cut your hair" to "You will never succeed, it's too big a leap for you." Thank them for bringing your beliefs to light. As you clear these beliefs, one by one, you clear the way for the more powerful YOU to emerge. Every person in life is an angel of guidance for your soul's healing journey.

People will always speak on subjects where you hold guilt or self-criticism. When you become okay about you, how you are, and what you do, others will be okay as well. They are reflecting the insecurities you hold in consciousness. Bring all insecurity to Light. Monitor how you feel hearing the words of others.

Are you also listening to your own words? What are you saying to other people? Individuals also appear in your life so you can give them advice, teach them, and minister to them. Although every word said may be valuable for them, they are really intended for the self. The reason you are given an opportunity to speak is so that you have the ability to hear advice you really need. You teach what you need to learn. Everything you say to others is what you are really saying to yourself. Every word of praise, support, love, and kindness, and every word of criticism, anger, ill will, and hate—it's all yours! Every piece of advice, recommendations, and prayers—yours too! They are all for you. You give what you need to get. The other showed up for you to grow in awareness. This is self-realization. Thank them and listen to what you are saying.

You cannot see in another what does not first exist within the self. Your judgments of others clearly illustrate the judgments you hold about yourself. These may be completely hidden from you, but realize you are a creature of projection. Lenses and filters are embedded within you that project your movie outward. Your greatest gifts are those individuals and experiences that are urging you to remove the lens and discard the filters. You are being blessed in this way, so that you can be one with the blessing. You are here to make a difference, to see the difference between reality and illusion, truths and lies, love and fear, self and Self. Your capacity to see and make a difference in the lives of others and in your own is the walk of the soul.

When you have really delved into your inner landscape and cleared away the debris, there will come moments where you no longer need to hear the praise of others. The specialness that others feel you are will not be necessary. You will no longer rely upon other's lips to affirm your beauty, your magnificence, and your majesty. It is because the moment will arise where you are ready to claim those truths for yourself. You will have grown to the point where you no longer need validation outside of yourself. Your "enoughness" becomes self-evident. You recognize you are beautiful, magnificent, and Divine. And it is all Go(o)d.

People are your mirrors in their behavior and their words. These mirrors are precious gifts because they let you know where you are in need of clearing beliefs and behaviors. Embrace life's incredible array of gifts, so that what no longer serves flows out of you. Be the container, fill and empty yourself. Fill and empty again and again in continual awareness of your rhythm. Do not allow anything to sit for too long. Do not let the container become stagnant and cloudy. Allow for cyclical moments of emptiness, of pure space. Do not view emptiness as a need to refill too quickly. Nor should you perceive the vacancy as an excuse to rush into fullness, especially in a haphazard way that does not serve the highest. Space and vacancy refine and recalibrate the evolutionary process for greater allowance and receiving. Be the essence of both spectrums. You are actually all of it, that which is the sacred space, holding the space, and surrounding it. Be the air outside of the container, that which connects and embraces all that it is surrounded by. This is communion and community. From this sacred impulse, you have come as one and all, the space between one and all, and the space surrounding one and all while also containing all of it.

Each individual is separate but One. Each is unique but the same. Every purpose and plan, ultimately the same, has a unique illustration. You and every person are pages of a great book. Each one is an individual story of tragedy and triumph, love and fear, pain and pleasure, success and failure, human and spirit. Each one is a story that must be imagined, written, read, and brought to life. But all of the stories unite in one sacred text. You are a sacred text of the One. You are the word manifest. You are creation that has created itself. Live your story, but know your origins are within One sacred story of LOVE made manifest and unified. Clarify, raise, and refine the story of Divinity through you.

Within your story there is truth. Then, there is greater truth. Finally there is TRUTH, DIVINE INFINITE TRUTH. Do not get caught up in your version of the illusion. Do not take things as truth because someone told you it was so, or because it has been that way for lineages. Whenever you feel the need to prove your point, state your case, or find evidence in support of your cause you are trying to convince yourself. Those moments hold an opportunity to go from what you perceive as truth to a deeper knowledge of the truth to the ultimate TRUTH beyond what most human minds have been privy to before this point. Truth states itself and is confident in that place. TRUTH connects and beholds all things. It does not judge, divide, fight, or cause fear. Truth is all encompassing. Truth is felt deeply inside, at your very core.

Be in full reflection. Reflect inward on what you desire, hold sacred, dream of, value, and love. Look around you. Look at who is around you and why. Be the reflection in the outer world of exactly the things you most desire to see. Be that desire in word, thought, and action. Be sacred in your steps. Live that dream today. Value yourself and everyone you come in contact with.

Love deeply. Love yourself. Love your life. Love the people in your life, for all they bring to it, in positivity and negativity. Love the conditions of your world. Love the human condition. Only when you accept where you are can something new unfold. Find your neutrality. There will always be people in your life to show you where you are, where you must go, and what you have not been able to see.

Janet's Story

Janet had been in a difficult marriage for quite some time. She had done everything possible to help her husband Jonathan and keep the marriage together. Jonathan accumulated several addictions over the years. Initially, he was working too many hours. Then he began drinking. Smoking followed. Janet came in for coaching because she suspected pornography and infidelity. She was tired and fed up.

Initially she walked into my office to find out how to help him, to try once again to save her marriage. It took a bit of a discussion to help her realize she could only help herself. Although his addictions were affecting her life, his issues were not her problem to solve. She had to come to greater understanding of how to help and change herself. However, she felt her husband would not be very supportive in her do so.

We cannot help anyone but ourselves. Based on what was mirroring in her world, Janet had a lot of hidden issues that needed addressing. It was very clear that she was not even aware of them. She was so busy looking outside and pointing a finger she had never taken the time to go inside. I would help her learn to see the outside as a complete reflection of her Self on the inside.

After three months of coaching, Janet began having some breakthroughs. She had been completely disconnected from her body and emotions for quite a long time.

"Janet, if you could use single words to describe your husband, what would you say?"

"Weak, selfish, smokestack, absent, sick." She spoke from outside of her body. It was closed and rigid. Her voice seemed distant and unfeeling.

"I want you to imagine that he is all of these things to show you how you are . . . or, how you feel about yourself."

Sitting up a little straighter and agitated by the mere suggestion, "Well, I do not do any of the things he engages in. I was not raised in that manner. I am a little offended at the suggestion."

"Bear with me for a minute. Let's look at each of those words. Just consider if there is a place in your life where you do these things to yourself, or someone else. Close your eyes and breathe so that you can hear your inner voice, without the distraction of the mind. I want you to imagine that you are sitting across from yourself. That 'you' is the one whose voice you are speaking. She is the one that has had to be too strong, too giving, and too unselfish for the sake of others and she is tired. In fact she is exhausted. Speak for her. Right now, you are the only friend she has got, the only hope she has left. I will say a word and you say what first comes to her mind. Now breathe. Take another two deep breaths focusing into her heart space. How are you weak?"

A slight tremble crossed her lips as her head tilted toward the floor. She adjusted her legs. Her eyes were closed, but her body was seeing very clearly. "I am too weak to leave this relationship. I am afraid of being on my own." A tear trickled down her left cheek, followed by another, and another. We processed through the layer of sadness that had arisen. The hard outer shell had been cracked and healing could begin. I moved to the next word.

"How have you been absent?"

"I guess I am here physically but I have emotionally left. We live very different lives and hardly see each other. I have been absent to my own needs. I have been absent to his real needs." I could see that realization, instead of rationalization, was starting to take hold.

"Can you tell me how you are sick?"

"I am sick and tired of living this life. I am sick of picking up after him. I am sick of cleaning up his messes. I am sick of pretending to people that everything is alright. I am sick of smiling and being a good wife. I am sick of my husband. I am sick of him. I am sick of him. I am sick of him! Oh my God, I am . . ." She burst into tears. Finally her body softened. The wall she had been holding up for many years had a break through it. There would be a long way to go, but she had hit awareness and was walking into acceptance. After a bit of processing, we continued.

"How are you a smokestack?"

Redness began creeping up her neck. "My neck gets red when I am upset. I can feel it now. I don't know, but I feel a lot of anger in this moment. I am so angry at him. I hate how he has treated me. This was not what we promised each other when we got married. I am angry for how he has turned away from me, how he has hurt me repeatedly without care." We processed through layers of anger.

Janet was opening to herself, probably for the first time in decades. She was following her impulses. She was connecting to her body and emotions.

"How are you selfish?"

"I do not know. I keep giving my all in this marriage. If anything I am giving too much. I am not a selfish person."

It was clear by her last statement she had a real judgment around being considered selfish. "You give your all to him you say?"

"Yes. My all and more."

"So, that must be exhausting and time-consuming."

"It is. I am always tending to him and it takes a lot of time. I do not have time for friends, or taking care of myself, or anything."

"That is pretty selfish of you to not share yourself. It is really selfish to not share yourself and your needs with YOU. How could you be more selfish for yourself instead of against yourself? Is that what Jonathan is really here to show you?"

"Wow . . . I never looked at it that way. I never considered selfish behavior to be those things. You are right; there is a lot in me that needs attention. I need to work on me. It's okay for me to be selfish in that way?" And with that a small smile formed, one that came from deep in her heart. "It is. I see now it is actually necessary."

Janet was moving toward healing, empowerment, and knowing all of who she really was. And her husband was the part of her that appeared as the message, the catalyst, the angel . . . the gift. As a soul, he loved her enough to endure the experience he chose for the sake of her soul growth and evolution. Can you imagine the depth of love that takes? Can you comprehend the degree of Oneness that existed before this embodiment and separation occurred as an experience of individuals in Earth School.

Projection Healing Exercise

Keep a journal of the things you say to others and the things others say to you. Then spend twenty minutes a day reflecting on one or two of those. Close your eyes. Scan where in your experience you behave in this way. Where in your body do you feel it? Feel into it. Love into it until you feel a shift. Breathe into it.

Look microscopically at yourself. These must be moments of radical honesty. This is work for deep excavation and purging. Discover where these behaviors appear and the people and places they touch.

Write how these behaviors serve you and what you gain from them. All behaviors serve in some way. They are either serving to keep you small, limited, unloved, and proving of your dramatic stories, or they are serving to empower, enliven, strengthen, and create new visions. Once you have determined the intention of the old behavior, choose a new intention and behavior. This will take discipline, but you can do it. As you discover this behavior in yourself and change it, the "other" will also shift in some way.

Do the work towards awareness and acceptance. Know that there could be other layers of this that still need to be found, but for now, you got what you were ready for. Remember, this is an exercise which means you have to stretch and flex. Stretch out of who you are and flex into who you desire to become.

Be open to your flexibility—your flex ability. You can do, be, or have anything your sacred heart desires. Flex ability occurs when you say YES to stretching beyond who you know yourself to be. It is when you say YES to actions and choices that inspire you, but which might scare the wits out of you. It is your YES to living and loving bigger than you ever dreamed possible. It is YES to discovering the hidden potential that you know is there but have been holding back. It is your YES to working all the muscles that you have not put into full use in the past. FLEX is "Feeling Like Experiencing X-traordinary Ability." Work it out. Stretch. Now Flex!

Have gratitude for the individual that showed you to yourself. Forgive yourself for any judgments you may have about you, them, or this. Have gratitude for yourself and your commitment to healing. Repeat the process when the additional layers appear. As you lift the burdens of the past, the real YOU will emerge Light and free to be.

Always approach new moments by asking yourself, "What step would I take today, if I were brave? What would I do if I had no fear?" Living from this position will hold the energy for continued transformation. There will be moments where you have to fake it till you make it, but how do you think those you admire got to where they are? We are not born ready. We prepare and ready ourselves to be born again and again. Life will begin shifting in powerful ways.

Experience Experiencing Experience

You, as experience, can express in many different ways. A circumstance or experience will show up for you in your world, but it will include objects and components to help you expand your perspective of Self and the situation at hand. You are always being asked to broaden your view and connection to the rest of humanity.

The entire world is at your disposal to be experienced. How much are you willing to engage as experience experiencing itself? Do you watch what is happening around you and then walk away unattached because you do not desire to touch it? That is not experience experiencing. That is not even a human experiencing, even though it may feel that way. This version of experience is no more than an interactive video game where you are the player watching a screen. The game is playing and touching everything, you are not. It's like being a fish in a fishbowl. You see everything, but it cannot affect you and you do not affect it.

However, the reason that experiences—also known as challenges, obstacles, triumphs, and ease—appear is because of the random connection of your interaction. You desire connection, but some part of you is either afraid of it or feels unworthy. There is no need to live behind a wall of glass. The things you fear happening will occur anyway, connection or no connection, simply because fear exists. It is better to leap into experience, walking with the fear or unworthiness. Only by walking with and through them will you discover they are false illusions. Challenges and obstacles are occurring to get you to feel, engage, and connect to parts of your Self that have been pushed away. Triumph and ease appear to assist in anchoring more into Go(o)d feelings. You are being called to immerse your Self in the experience of life. In doing so, without getting bogged down in any one experience, you will realize the experience of living out your life. In reality, life experiencing is living through you. You think you are loving life, but actually life is "in love" with you. You are not doing anything with your life; life is being with you as a creation of itself. You do not breathe to have life, but breath gives life unto and reveals through you. You need only open to being "presence" to the experience so that life can inhale and exhale deeply through you. In ceasing presence and participation, experiencing wanes.

When disconnected, bored, or tired, the breath will be shallow. It will be short, high in the chest, and engaged mindlessly. You would experience working too hard for life—in fact, working for Love. Submersing your Self in life, experiences as holding the Self down and back. When something is submerged, the natural response is to hold the breath and go into constriction and fear. Submersion is forced and fights and works to survive.

Experience experiencing itself is asking for something greater. Move from submersion to immersion. Immersion is by choice, it flows and thrives. Love does not ask you to work for it, love just is. Relax into it.

Let Love, let life, let breath in to guide, fill, and nurture you. Immersion is simply falling into the space and being held by that space.

When you are engaged and immersed completely in oneness, notice how your breathing deepens. Life deeply breathes and creates through you, vitality increases and life force is stronger. Inhales are deep, expanding the torso. Exhales are broad, swelling outward as resonant Ahhhh's. Needs flow in and away in synchronicity. Although the mind wants to identify as being an object such as a human being, you are really experience. Experience experiencing itself consciously acknowledges and allows life in this way. Let go of trying to live life. You need only to be life, you need only to feel aliveness. All need only be continuously in the field of love. This is evolution.

Engagement of life in this manner will yield a broadened perspective. You will not only see all of the things life expresses as, but that you are that expression. Each moment is an experience; nothing is separate. Each part requires the other to be a whole experience. A flower cannot have fragrance without the engagement of inhaling scent. A mountain cannot be regal without being gazed upon. A puppy cannot be soft and sweet without a presence to witness, hold, and caress it. You are the experiencing. All else is apparatus appearing for the sake of experience experiencing itself. All that is experience is what you have designed to know as experience experiencing itself in infinite evolution and expansion.

The Eight Evolutionary Stages of Experience Experiencing Itself into Infinity Possibility

Experience experiencing itself has eight evolutionary stages that are an ever-expanding loop of infinity possibility. These are identified as stages of soul development as the earthly realm into God Being.

Stage ONE	Soul Contraction	Creative Capacity	Creator	God Self

Stage One is the expansion of the God Self experiencing its creative capacity. God Self moves into a Soul Contraction, meaning it dives inward and expands, like an inhale and exhale. The Soul experiences itself as Creative Capacity by being the Creator aspect of the God Self. In doing so, another "contraction" occurs where the soul chooses to have a "contract" for a greater experience as play in Earth School. This contraction and contract is the birthing of a new earth experience as the Earthly Self, also known as Stage Two.

Stage TWO	Energy	Earth	Environment	Earthly Self

The Earthly Self is the experience of Energy forming all facets of a world of experiencing. It is Godhead experiencing itself as an environment. Creative Capacity fills this earth space with a multitude of replications of itself. The Soul Contraction allows for a deep inhale and exhale to birth land, seas, animals, and wildlife. Stage Two is the setting or platform and the environmental positioning for the continuation of the Divine Essence. The environment will include the tribe and the birth of the soul for a tangible earthly experience.

Stage THREE	Wound	Amnesiam	Victimhood	False Self

Stage Three is the "what" and "how" happenings, in addition to experiencing reaction or response to that happening. Experience is experiencing survival. The Earthly Self has birthed into an environment of experiences and, in doing so, identifies that as separate instead of seeing it as the experience of itself. It has encountered "amnesiam," Am not I AM, the antithesis of I Am or I AM that I AM. It is the experience of forgetting God Self as experience experiencing. Instead, the soul contracts and identifies with a wounded nature stemming from a perception of separation and duality. However, this contractual inhale is the expansion into the False Self who anchors in the experience of victimhood. This exhale also provides an earthly experience of the wound, which would lead the Self inward again.

Stage FOUR	Reflector	Dark Night Dawning	Healing	Hue-man Self

Stage Four is experience as Reflector, providing the opportunity of transitioning the wound, experienced as the dark night, into the dawn of healing. As experience experiences itself moving from unconscious to more conscious, the unfolding contraction is the birthing of the Human Self, the Hue-Man Self or Light Man Self. The experience of dawning brings the experience of Light. Contractual inhalation brings the awareness of Light to the experience of exhalation as Light, evolving Self to Stage Five.

Stage FIVE	Witness	Observer	Awakening	Wisdom Self

Stage Five is experience experiencing itself as awakening and expansion into the Wisdom Self. The Witness watches the experience play out as a deeper layer of growth and healing is being experienced. Witness holds within an Observer experiencing service as midwife to the birthing experience as Hue-man Self, Light Man Self. The Observer feels and thinks into what is being witnessed from a neutral perspective. The Observer engages the awakening for the expansion of the Wisdom Self into its Stage Six experience as ministry.

Stage SIX	Service	Connection	Transformation	Compassionate Self

Stage Six is the gateway for the Wisdom Self to be experiencing itself as a ministry, sacred space of the word. The experience of Service as experiencing connection through ministering and teaching creates the experience of transformation for the teacher and the student, the minister and the listener. We are all teachers and ministers. Acts of service engage the expansion of the Wisdom Self into the birthing of the Compassionate Self. Experience experiencing accesses the Compassionate Self, recognizing itself as a loving gift to be shared with others.

This is the breath of the Universe deepening and widening as inhalations and exhalations of conscious awareness expanding.

Stage SEVEN	Oneness	Community	Evolution	Loving Self

Stage Seven engages the Compassionate Self into the experience of Oneness experiencing Service and Community. This births the Loving Self, which has an expanding ability of holding an overview. The Loving Self experiences a broadened understanding as to why things happen as they do. Here is experience experiencing itself as the "I" watching others, without the need to teach, minister, serve, or save.

The Loving Self experiences its mere presence as enough. Here is celebration of experience and acknowledgment of the essence of Self as Godhead. This experience of Self-Realization enLightens the human and illuminates the soul, uniting the inhale and exhale as a singular circular breath. As the breath deepens and expands, the infinite returns to center, the central point of all things.

Stage EIGHT	Allness	Creation	Transcendence	Infinite Self

Stage Eight is the gathering of Allness to a point of rest at the intersection of all movement. Experience has its soul review to reflect upon the experience of creation and its transcendence. The Infinite Self is the movement and the stillness, the contraction and the expansion, the inhale and the exhale, the space between and around. It has no end and no beginning. It has no judgment or will. It simply is possibility.

EXPERIENCE EXPERIENCING ITSELF

	Experience	Experiencing	Experience	Expanding Consciousness
Stage ONE	Soul Contraction	Creative Capacity	Creator	God Self
Stage TWO	Energy	Earth	Environment	Earthly Self
Stage THREE	Wound	Amnesiam	Victimhood	False Self
Stage FOUR	Reflector	Dark Night Dawning	Healing	Hue-man Self
Stage FIVE	Witness	Observer	Awakening	Wisdom Self
Stage SIX	Service	Connection	Transformation	Compassionate Self
Stage SEVEN	Oneness	Community	Evolution	Loving Self
Stage EIGHT	Allness	Creation	Transcendence	Infinite Self

The eight stages are the endless movement of infinity, as expressed creative capacity, ever-growing, ever-evolving, energetic agents of experience in consciousness. Experience only has one purpose, and that is to experience itself. It is never looking for an end destination because it only experiences never ending. Therefore, you only have one true purpose and that is to experience. Although you set goals, dreams, and destinations, they are only part of an endless loop of the infinite possibility of continual experience and expansion.

We also do this on a grand scale as cities, states or nations, continents, or oceans. Each performs its cycle of Godhead falling and rising in the cycle of infinity, collaborating in the continual involution and evolution of the all-ness that is.

Events in the world are generated in order to have a collective experience of involution and evolution. These illustrate mass mindedness within the eight-stage process. Each person experiences as an individual, yet we are at oneness when viewing the horror of terrorism, the compassion of service, or the excitement of celebration. In that moment, you are collective experience experiencing the creation of collective consciousness experiencing itself. These grander versions of experience, which will range from experiences of terrorism to that of unconditional service, are what are held in various stages of infinite expansion toward different points of infinity.

The Nature of Reality

Nature speaks constantly. Through shapes, color, textures, smells, and varied animal life, it provides expression about the world and your life. One of the most powerful signs nature offers comes from cycles. The illustration of beginnings and endings, birth and death, depletion and renewal is everywhere in life, but still we forget it is only the process of change. Required for the process of growth and evolution, change will always be a natural expression. The only difference is the degree to which it is resisted.

Change can feel as if it is forced upon an individual. By allowing what desires to arise to flow naturally, the path will be easier. If trying to control or harness change, the path will feel challenging and painful along the way. The Universe teaches about the constant of change through the changing seasons. You will see it is a gradual allowing. The change of one season to another is not abrupt or instantaneous; it is a process of graduation. Winter blossoms into springtime. Summer turns into fall. Not only do they clearly illustrate birthing anew, playfully basking, releasing, and stillness, the seasons tell us when to do it. But the seasons are also guiding in a deeper way, one that is intentional and directive.

Have you ever wondered why certain experiences occur at specific times in your life, in a specific season? It is because the cycle of that experience is being revealed to you. It could be a job, relationship, creation, or behavior. Notice when things begin in your life. Notice when they are asking you to play and bask and be inspired. Be cognizant of when they are asking you to let go and of what needs to be let go. Listen carefully when you are being requested to be open, bare, and still. Each piece of you, as you, as endeavor or as experience, has a cycle and rhythm.

The seasons will tell you your next step. The spring is a time of new beginnings and birthing. The summer is the season of basking, playing, and resting. The autumn brings a time for letting go and change. Finally winter requests that you bare yourself, become still, and go within.

If beginning something new, allow the season to guide you as to how to be. As you move through the year, the seasons will guide you as to the changes being asked for, as moments of success and challenges arise. In this way, you are not in reactivity but rhythmic activity. You are uniting into oneness to have it assist in the flow and integration of arising experiences. Regardless of what you are experiencing in your life or when it began, evaluate things from different perspectives based on the season you are in. The energies at various times of the year will support the moves that need to be made if you will allow for rhythm, connection, and conversation. You do not have to believe me, just try it.

Below are brief chartings of what the seasons are communicating to you. Whatever the issue, implement this nature into your thoughts, words, feelings, and actions and see how differently you feel and what arises. In releasing a little of the control and by knowing the Universe has your back, you will find the Universe is not only talking to you, but walking with you. It is not only holding the space, it has created the space.

THE SYMBOLS OF SPRING

Flowers	Open yourself, show yourself
Green grass	Grow your foundation in the Heart
Warm Air	Feel secure in yourself
Sunshine	Express your Power
Rich soil, flowing water	Receive nourishment
Baby animals	Move from a place of innocence
Fragrance of Newness	Breathe it all in

Let the seasons guide the steps of your life, providing an illustrative expanse of what needs to be allowed. Spring symbolizes a time to open, express, and be nurtured. It is your time to receive who you are. This is a moment of birthing anew and awakening to the wonder and innocence experience allows. New bulbs and blooms also suggest joyful acknowledged expression of that wonder. Feel secure in the place of vulnerability because you are abundantly cared for and loved. There is a strong sense of community in spring as flowers blossom, insects and birds hover about, and all of nature comes alive. There is grand celebration in the air. Have this feeling in your life. When you can receive, you have a greater ability to give and shine through with your magnificence.

THE SYMBOLS OF SUMMER

Long days	Stretch, extend yourself
Birds fly to habitats	Return to Center
Dry air	Allow & engage deeper breath
Humid air	Allow & engage more emotion
Thunderstorms, storms	Feel the inner swirling, inner upset
Gnats, mosquitos	Notice irritation, give generously
Butterflies, dragonflies	Coming transformation & change

Summer symbolizes a time to bask in what you have put out into the world. It is the moment of rest. Fully reflect so you can see who you are in the full light of day. Stretch yourself and engage more deeply with the Self so you are prepared for any coming transformation. This is the Light equivalent to winter. This is the time to be in the world and not of it.

THE SYMBOLS OF AUTUMN

Falling leaves	Let go, release what is dying
Reds, oranges, golds	Trust, heal, find your power
Cool crisp air	Wake up to yourself
Ripening berries	Things have completed
Seeds	Time for new seeds in life
Harvests	Have gratitude for what came
Birds migrate	Ground, strengthen your core

Autumn symbolizes a time to reap what you have sown. You are the harvest that all can be nourished by and rejoiced in. It is a moment to be creative, colorful, and expressive. You create change for yourself and others. Have gratitude as things find completion and new seeds are planted.

Winter symbolizes a time of going into the cave and nestling in the quietness. It is the time for the renewal of energies, a time to be dormant and create space again in deep opening to prepare for another flowering to come. This is a time to be in your inner world and completely of it.

Allow the subtle clues of the seasons to be a guiding force of "being" in the world. So often individuals are questioning the subject of "being" when it is adequately displayed all around. Being is misconstrued as not doing anything. This is not the case. As nature illustrates in its being, things keep changing, growing, evolving, beginning, and ending. Being is the expression of presence that is brought to what is being asked for in the moment. The seasons, along with everything else in nature, are wise teachers and guides. They speak the language of allowing "now." In that presence of now, there need be nothing else.

THE SYMBOLS OF WINTER

Snow	Visualize & crystallize forms
Cold temperatures	Go completely within for answers
Barren trees	Be open, vulnerable, and bare
Quiet forests	Listen for answers
Ice	Stop all movement. Slow actions
Animals hibernate	Rest, renew, sleep, rejuvenate
Long dark nights	Do your inner work and healing

Animals Speak

One of the most magical experiences of synchronicity and conversation is with the animal kingdom. Love comes packaged in such beautiful ways and one of the most diverse and magnificent is the animal kingdom. I am always joyfully surprised at what shows up in my world. Animals and animal spirits teach a great deal about the Self and the grand capacities it possesses. You hold the essence, characteristics, and wisdom of each animal alive. Within you are the aspects that they represent. In addition, a greater universal wisdom times your meetings with these wonderful guides in the exact moments you are in need of their traits. This is a different form of medicine, a kind of spirit medicine that feeds the soul.

In the moment you have lost your way, you will discover a string of insects, reptiles, aquatics, or animals will make their way into your experience. Most people completely bypass the significance of these creatures appearing in front of them. But what if nothing, absolutely nothing, is random? What if, within your very matrix, you have programmed a signal to call in your unique animal totems? They arrive to awaken you to a decision, choice, or behavior more in alignment with your higher good.

Perhaps, when in moments of depression, despair, hopelessness, or pain, the exact animal essence you need appears to pull you up and out. Have you ever noticed during moments of tremendous change, and oftentimes pain, dragonflies flutter across your path? Have you noticed when making significant transformational choices regarding personal power, butterflies dance about? What do you find when too busy, always working, and always running? Do not be surprised if you have an ant issue in your home or at work. It is also amazing how dogs find their owners just before the owner is about to embark on a challenging period or dark night of the soul. Dogs are the representation of unconditional self-love. Animals support discovery concerning the invisible worlds of the Self.

Learn the language of their behaviors in the physical world. They are teaching you how to be. Just watch them. They exhibit the exact qualities you must enact in your current experience to shift that situation. The Native Americans and many other indigenous people know this. The Western world has lost touch with its wiser, instinctive counterpart. Every animal is endowed with a powerful spirit, talent, and medicine. Their greatest message asks that an individual's passionate and boldly free desire to experience be activated. Allow your wild, instinctive nature to roam free.

You must understand that animals choose you. It is no more random than anything else in this earthly matrix. We do not choose them. They know when to come. It is the law of attraction, but more so the original Law of Spirit.

The Law of Spirit states that all that exists will manifest into the forms that are of resonant frequencies for the purposes of continual awareness of I AM into perpetual Oneness. These forms that manifest, such as in animals, are linked to higher nature and soul essence. In reality, varying degrees of frequency exist because awareness of infinite Oneness already exists. However, the various aspects must rise into alignment with those aspects to manifest those forms. All other Laws of Spirit fall beneath this overarching umbrella Law as guiding principles for the manner in which alignment curriculum manifests. Communication in this manner demands respect for each form and the journey onward and upward.

Animals are to be honored and revered for the medicine that they bring to life, as a tangible aspect of the Law of Spirit. You will find all kinds of animals enter your life, from the exotic to those viewed as common household pets. Don't forget, they are choosing you. They can utilize any means of manifestation to speak to you: an image, paper, stone, wooden carving, picture, postcard, statue, or real life. Do not discount their appearance in your life. They are speaking to you. Animals are the Universe speaking to you about YOU.

Household pets are especially significant. Consider them an extension of your spirit. They are here as guides, teachers, and surrogates. They will guide you in how to act, feel, and live. They will teach you how you are. They will be surrogates for many of your embedded wounds and hidden wounds, manifesting dis-ease on your behalf to protect you.

Those you "choose" as pets have come specifically to you and for you. They chose you well before you found them. They will always have deep personal meaning and connection to your soul journey. They will illustrate their wisdom but are also here to express you. These animals will illustrate your issues to help you see where you need to focus and clear. Their bodies will hold symptoms for you. Their behaviors will show you the patterns within yourself you cannot see. They love you enough to carry a lot for you. These animals are intimately linked to you and your soul journey of healing and growth. Acknowledge them as the angelic beings that they are.

Victor & Cindi's Story

An interesting story developed with a couple that I have known most of my life. We attended their wedding and became good friends. As I learned the language of the Universe, this revealed as one of the most profound examples of how our stories play out right in front of us. It also illustrates how the world around people serves to protect, heal, and guide them.

Victor and Cindi decided to get a puppy after having been married two years. Victor came home with a cognac-colored male Italian Greyhound they named Adonis. This dog had personality, loved people, was restless, and needy for affection. No one realized that he was the mirror representation of Victor. The dog was very active and restless. Six months later in an attempt to keep the dog company, Victor and Cindi decided to get a second dog.

They wanted to select breeds that would suit their lives at the time. Since they were living in a small, two-bedroom apartment, the dogs needed to fit their lifestyle. The criteria: the dogs could not shed, should not bark, and would remain small in stature. Little did they realize this would also become what Victor and Cindi's marital lives would imitate. Projection can reflect in many ways.

Cindi would choose the second dog—or so she thought. Cleopatra was a black and grey brindle whippet. She caught Cindi's eye right away. In the pet store, the whippet faced the back of the cage, her face buried in the corner. Something about the pup drew Cindi in. All of the other puppies had their faces at the fronts of cages, performing and excitedly jumping around. The whippet was not interested in the people, much less performing.

Cindi stood in front of the cage, unable to tear away from the tiny creature inside. The whippet slowly looked back at Cindi, briefly stared into her eyes, and then nestled her face back into the corner. Cindi remembers a voice within saying, "She is yours . . . she is you." At the time Cindi let the thought flutter by, brushing it off without consideration. She immediately decided this was the dog she had to have.

While completing paperwork, the pet store clerk told the couple she was full breed but had been severely abused for four months of her life. The whippet had been unresponsive, sitting in the corner of the cage most of the time in the pet store. He wanted to make certain they still wanted her. Cindi did.

Upon reaching home, the two dogs seemed to bond well with each other. However, their personalities were quite distinct and codependent. Adonis, the social one, was beautiful and always seeking attention. Cleopatra would feed this by constantly grooming him, licking his face and ears on a nightly basis. She would let Adonis lay across her hips and back legs as if her body was his pillow.

Cleopatra was shut down and reserved. Rather than going to people, she would wait for them to come to her. She had a regal heir about her, which could make her appear snobbish. She was not like other dogs; she would not lick or kiss. She did not know how. She had never felt love. From the time she was born, she had been abused and neglected. Adonis would sit on her back hips and legs, pinning her down. He would also alert Cindi as to when Cleopatra needed to go outside. The whippet would just follow along.

Cindi never connected her own degree of childhood abuse and neglect to the selection of the whippet. It was not until years later when I pointed out the symbolism that all the dots came together for her. The relationships for both Cindi and the whippet continued the pattern of abuse from others. It also became apparent how codependency within the relationship mirrored through the dogs.

Looking back, it becomes evident that the dogs were playing out Victor and Cindi's lives. Early on, Adonis developed seizures after a head injury. Seizures illustrate a fear of life. Because it was triggered by a head injury, it means fears stemming from the mind. Victor dealt with severe anxiety and depression and Adonis was the mirror for that.

Over time, because of the pressure on her legs from Adonis, Cleopatra developed hip dysplasia and inflammation of the lower spine. She also experienced clouding of the eyes. The hip issues speak of suppressed creative capacity and challenged relationship to the self and others. The lower back illustrates lack of support and built up anger. The eyes denote clouded vision or direction. Cindi was challenged to express herself fully and lost sight of her own dreams for the sake of those around her. There was built up anger and resentment for the lack of support she always had felt. Victor and Cindi's lives clearly mirrored the same emotional and psychological issues with some of the same health issues arising as well.

During the marriage, Cindi was never able to fully express her creative nature. She felt disconnected from others, remained isolated, and felt challenged in connecting to her own emotions and vision. Victor fell into addictions which required treatment. His fears would always get the better of him as he was controlled by a strong sense of inadequacy and worthlessness. The couple experienced many ups and downs. The dogs did as well by becoming the energetic conduits for Victor and Cindi's individual and codependent dysfunction.

The dogs grew to the ages of fourteen. A moment came when Adonis could not walk well, was experiencing slight dementia, and the effects of old age. His sight and hearing had deteriorated. He was physically present, but the rest of him was absent. The couple inquired as to whether he needed to be put down.

Cleopatra was having a hard time walking. Her hip degeneration was causing weakness in the legs. Victor and Cindi knew she might be depressed without Adonis and might also need to be put down as her quality of life seemed to be compromised.

The vet advised that both dogs were experiencing rapid deterioration and a date was arranged for the following week. Upon returning home, Adonis passed quickly. He happened into the path of a car where his skull was crushed. This happened to coincide with Cindi's sudden realization she no longer wanted to be in the relationship. Victor moved out. The couple had mutually decided to go their separate ways.

Cindi thought Cleopatra would experience depression. However, she had more spring in her legs than ever. Instead of being depressed, she seemed happy. She was running again when she had not in many months. Her tail was wagging again. She was feeling a taste of freedom. Cindi called the vet and cancelled the appointment to put the dog to sleep. Adonis's moving on was Victor's moving on. Cleopatra's resurgence of energy was Cindi's renewed energy.

The couple's initial requirements also played out in their lives: no shedding, no barking, and small in stature. These two individuals had been challenged in shedding their emotions. Midway through the marriage both breeds, which are not known to bark, began barking, illustrating to both owners the need to state their voices because they had been silent, not expressing their true feelings or needs. Finally the requirement to be small in stature was exactly what they each did within the marriage. Since divorcing, both people are thriving, happy, and expressing in a manner true to their soul expression.

Coincidence? Synchronicity? Reflections? Messages? Mirrors? Be willing to see what you have not seen. Test it out in your own life. Your animal will reflect your inner landscape. It will also reflect your outer life. What is your animal telling you about you? What health issues is it carrying for you?

7

Guides

Every individual is here as a teacher, a minister, and a guide. In the course of life, we cross many others that have lived similar circumstances. These opportunities allow us to step out of our story and use it to support others in their personal journey. In the process, our own wounds heal.

You are a teacher, a minister. Those you teach appear so that you may teach what you need to hear. In doing so, you become the angel for their experience and the healing of your Self. How will you answer this call? How will you be different? Who are you speaking to? How are you touching? Anyone that claims to have it all together is not a "real" teacher. Each individual is here to learn and grow and share the wisdom from integrated growth, only to encounter more change and obstacles for new lessons to teach. Remove your masks; let your students see you and know you. Be willing to be vulnerable, open, and transparent. Reveal the heart. This activates authentic, conscious healing and connection. There is no need to stand on a pedestal; it is lonely and dangerous up there. Come back down and be a part of experience experiencing.

As you take personal responsibility, you bring the world more towards oneness. When you choose to be more authentic in right word, right thought, and right action, you move into right living. Individual integrity brings the world into greater integrity. In taking the time to heal and reintegrate wholeness into personal experience, you heal your world of all of its ills. You become an angel to others.

The wisdom gained through experience is adorned with the angelic essence of compassion, kindness, and generosity when heart can meet heart in the same place. The simple act of recognition of one's own story within that of another renders energy waves of love and healing to the individual undergoing pain. For the one who has already experienced such a circumstance, the other is also a guide. They are holding the space and expression of the experience so that it can be witnessed again, this time without survival influences, without the depths of pain, and without the need to change anything. Those who need your teaching and your wisdom are also angels.

You have assistance on both, the seen and unseen realms. You can call in support for messages and guidance. Angels are readily available for this. They will always answer. They will always support you. They are your team. They are you.

My life reflects stories of pain and challenge. It also holds healing, growth, awareness, and acceptance. This combination gleaned wisdom, which I have been able to share with many. These students and listeners have been my angels as witness to my journey. They also served so I may hear myself, take in the lesson again, and integrate in a deeper way. I have been their angel in teaching, loving, and illustrating how to heal and grow. In the end it is experience as me and experience as you. The two come together as experience experiencing.

Speaking through Dreams

The Universe, as you, is speaking to you inside and out. The dream state is an inner state of dialoguing for guidance, clairvoyance, and resolution. It is not as much about what is in the dream as how the dream makes you feel. However, the symbolism of the dream takes the conversation a little deeper. Dreams are a link between Higher Self that is guiding creation and the Self that is creation. The outer landscape reflects what we hold unconsciously. The inner landscape uses dreams and references that trigger you to become aware, heal, and resolve the issues holding you hostage.

There are many dream books available to suggest meaning of different things that appear. Let the inquisitive mind explore these meanings, but do so after allowing the intuitive mind to have a go at it. You know more than you think you know. Dreams are a way to discover that innate knowledge.

The most important thing you need to understand about dreams is that everything in them is you. Regardless of what appears or whom appears, they are all you represented as a certain feeling or belief you have about that person or thing. That feeling or belief is what your dream-self is asking you to engage with. The people that appear in your dream represent the aspect of them that you hold within. You may or may not have previously noted that aspect about yourself. However, that is what they are here to show you. The animals and other things within the dream are illustrating the same. Settings illustrate a sense of where you feel you are in life, again a feeling such as: free, imprisoned, comfortable, in danger, on a tightrope, stressed, etc. Let the dreams tap into your feeling and intuitive nature. Dive into the movie that they are. Let them take you inside of yourself to discover and uncover what lives within.

The mind will always want to get involved first. However, begin with the heart. Remember, everything exists for you to have an experience. Approach this from that perspective. The mind is not a place of experience. It is a place of figuring out or toiling. The heart is for feeling, experiencing, and knowing. This is experience and you are the experiencing. The dream is in and of itself the deeper experience. Hence, this is a play of experience experiencing experience.

What dream do you seek? Do you desire to be the conscious dream or do you desire to be in the dreaming? Do you think it is too grand to be a fully awakened conscious dream? Too farfetched? Too crazy? Too much for you to have? Well, YOU are what dreams are made of.

Right now, you are the sleeping dreamer. However, you still hold your essence, imagination, creativity, inspiration, direction, intention, and affirmation. If you do the work, the inner work, heal yourself, love yourself, allow yourself, and have for yourself the knowing you deserve all that and more, you will manifest from awakening from a dream to being the awakened dreamer living a dream. Dare to be the dream because when you do, you are giving permission for YOU to be all of you! You are also allowing creation to place the blessing of itself in you, your hands, and your life.

How does one wake up to expansion, desire, and greatness? How does one become the dream? It has to start somewhere, and that place is in the ethers. Now dream again, within the sleeping dream. Daydream or dream at night. Get lost in your dreams. Anchor "in love" and then let your imagination and visualization soar. Dream on! The power of creation exists in, as, and through you. You can manifest from any level that you are. You can dream yourself . . . Up!

Experiencing "The Dream" within the Dream

➤ Upon awakening from the dream:

➤ Remain relaxed with your eyes closed and breathe.

➤ Anchor into the feelings that were activated through the dream.

➤ Do not analyze anything yet.

➤ Simply reflect upon the dream and see how different things feel.

➤ Allow the images that are of greater significance to pop out at you.

➤ Do not judge or analyze, just feel.

➤ After you have been in the feeling state for a while and remembered the dream, write the details down in a dream journal.

➤ Take three deep breaths and set an intention to interpret the dream that is supportive to your highest self and higher learning.

➤ Journal for twenty minutes if possible.

➤ Now to satisfy the mind, you may look up any symbolism in a dream book.

➤ If any awareness arises out of the exploration, add that to your journal.

➤ Dreams will typically reflect an issue that you are dealing with. They arise to open the perspective to a higher resolution.

➤ Upon completion of your interpretation of the dream, breathe in your revelations for eleven minutes to anchor them into the body.

Millicent's Story

A woman contacted me about what she called a "dark" spirit. "I have a new acquaintance—a seemingly gentle man—who has come to me twice now in spirit in a dark, unsettling, bordering on threatening, way. When I sleep, I'm often able to connect with my spirit, which occasionally interacts with others, usually family. But this interaction is unusual and after both experiences I awoke and thought, "I should fear him," yet I don't. I believe that's because I felt my beloved Granddaddy's spirit guided me to him. I feel that this man is tied to my destiny, but I don't know how. It is not a love interest. I feel that perhaps I'm supposed to encourage him to discover himself? He seems to have great power waiting to be tapped, but I wonder why it seems to be 'dark.' Perhaps the words 'troubled' or 'disturbed' are more appropriate than 'dark.' Can you help me interpret this dream?"

There were several things clear to me upon reading her inquiry. First of all, after waking, she "thought" she should fear him. This is the mind responding from past programming or belief systems. She later says some feeling told her she did not need to. That is the wisdom of the heart speaking. I responded quickly, easily seeing what was trying to reveal itself.

"Maybe, he is coming to show you yourself, an unseen aspect which, when brought to Light, will open a great power within YOU ready to be released and shared. Be open to see the 'dark' parts of yourself you have not seen or have judged. Bring them back home and integrate them into you with love, compassion, and forgiveness. There is only One, divided into many pieces and parts desiring to reveal Oneness. This man is a blessing being given to you. Ask him to reveal his gift. Embrace him, do not fear him. Pour love into the experience. Open your heart and stay anchored in the feelings of what subsequent dreams provide. He is you, as a guide in a different form."

Millicent responded quickly. "Yes! This is true. I have held back my power. I always try to be positive for everyone. I do not let myself ever express any of my negative or dark feelings or thoughts. I judge myself for those. I will now open to working with those sides of myself and will allow this guide to help me."

Dare to Dream the Daydream

Daydreaming also appears so you can move beyond who you are in the Dream. Do not limit yourself by what you see. Go by your feelings and follow the instincts that arise. You are here to dream the bigger dream. What dream do you seek? Do you think it's too grand? Too farfetched? Too crazy? Too much for you to have?

YOU are what dreams are made of. They are your essence, imagination, creativity, inspiration, direction, intention, and affirmation. If you do the work, the inner work, heal yourself, love yourself, allow yourself, and have for yourself the knowing you deserve all that and more, they will be the manifestation. Dare to dream because when you do, you give permission for you to be all of YOU! Allow creation to place the blessing of itself in you, your hands, and your life. It has to start somewhere, and that place is in the ethers. Get lost in your dreams. You must be dreaming! So dream on!

Manifesting the Dream through Daydreaming

➤ Relax and close your eyes.

➤ Anchor the attention into the heart.

➤ Breathe from the earth, inhaling through the feet up to the heart.

➤ Exhale from the heart up to the Universe.

➤ Inhale from the Universe back to the Heart.

➤ Exhale back down through the feet into the earth.

➤ Continue the breath evenly in this manner.

➤ Focus your sight into the third eye point, still with eyes closed.

➤ Begin daydreaming your desires.

➤ As you do so, feel into the desires. Know them as real.

➤ Allow images of greater significance to pop out at you.

➤ Do not judge or analyze, just feel.

➤ After you have been in the feeling state and anchored into the dream, write the details down in a vision journal.

➤ Take the time to focus on this dream on a daily basis. You have placed it into energetic form. Give it time to manifest physically.

➤ Monitor yourself so that thoughts, feelings, and actions each day are in the positive direction and supportive creation of your dream.

Louisa's Story

Louisa came to the realization that she had the ability to dream, but all she had had the experience of was broken dreams. She wanted to believe in dreams coming true, but had nothing to base that on. "Why do I hang onto broken dreams when my daydreams look so amazing? I want to be happy but do not know how. It seems like everywhere I go I receive messages to go for my dreams. But how do I know they will work out? I seem to just be chasing dreams but never catching any."

The Universe is trying to tell you that you can have what you want and more. Let go of what is broken, just place it aside. Maybe have two little boxes set up. Label one "Broken Dreams" and label the other "My Manifest Dreams." Write the dreams down and place them into the appropriate box to be released.

Sometimes people hold onto what is broken because they believe they need to have a job, they need to be broken. What better job than to fix things, right? Nothing in your life was ever broken. This was just a way to express your creative nature. Now it is time to discover the Divine nature of creativity. Instead of chasing dreams, sit in one. You know how, you did it last night. The same way you dream in the night, dream in the day. Dream it until the dream makes itself real. Breathe it to life. It will become real if you are following the steps to anchor it.

8

Signs

Have you ever been driving down the road and the exact song depicting how you were feeling began to play? Have you noticed that cards and random quotes appear specific to what you need in a certain moment? Have you ever come upon or been given a book that speaks to exactly where you were in that moment? Or have you ever gravitated toward a certain color or pattern repeatedly? Maybe a certain object keeps landing in front of you or you may even start to gather a specific collection. Perhaps a piece of art grabs your eye and you have to have it.

Signs are provided in a constant stream so that we can't help but see them. They come into our lives as purchases, gifts, and points of awareness. Signs are tangible items, placed in front of you, which are the pieces of your puzzle. This would include books, objects, artwork, songs, and color.

Artwork: In the Eye of the Beholder

Artwork is a key player in helping you see your story. You will naturally gravitate towards and only select what resonates with you. Artwork is very heart centered. Your focus will be directed to what speaks to your deepest longings. There is a part of you that already knows what you are set to encounter in your life, based on the mental and emotional trajectory you have in place. This part guides your selections in an attempt to communicate to you what is on the horizon. Peruse your home and get familiar with what is there. Those paintings, pictures, statues, and objects are not just taking up space. They are speaking to you. They are you.

Even if you hired a decorator to come in and design your home, the images on the walls or artistic pieces will still relate to your journey. There is no place that the oneness of spirit is not. The earthly matrix always brings you exactly what you need. Your home is no exception. Any place you reside will offer guidance. I have even found it staying in hotels. If I have gone for a specific purpose to an area, the pictures on the walls of the hotel room speak to why I am there. They will illustrate a theme that I am to know. Life is always working on your behalf. You need only be aware of its continual support and expression.

Look around your home. You will discover that your life has been depicted in pictures, statues, and gifts that have been purchased by you or given to you. These items reveal information about your relationships, obstacles, larger breakthroughs, and your soul journey. They will have meaning and give meaning to the journey when you turn and look back. This life chronicle will let you see that nothing has been a mistake, but is actually part of a grand design.

I remember the moment I realized my life story was depicted upon the walls of my home. I went from room to room matching up images with the experiences in my life. It was eerie how intricately my life journey was illustrated. The framed art had been purchased prior to the experiences, foretelling what was to come. Even the art others gave told my story. My husband and I had been given a Salvador Dali piece as a wedding gift. It was the story of our marriage. At the time, it seemed like just an interesting piece of art.

Objects d'art, statues, and figurines played a role as well. They described aspects of my life. There was a period of my journey I kept receiving frogs as gifts. I did not collect frogs. I had not asked for frogs. But I received frogs of all types, large and small, ceramic and stuffed, metal and glass, paper-mache and wooden. The frog symbolizes strength, adaptability, and creativity. All of these "hopped" into my life during a challenging period. They were telling me to access my strength, adapt to the changes that were coming, and create. My life fell apart during those two years but *11:11 Magazine* and my life's work birthed in that process as well. The frogs had come to usher that in.

At another point in my journey, I was forced to face all of the masks that I wore. Until then, I had not realized the degree of illusion I had created through masks. I remember when the many faces of me revealed themselves. I had gone to my son's room to put away laundry. The house was quiet and I was alone. I stowed his clothes in the bureau, except for one set of shirts.

As I came up from bending down over the dresser drawers, my head struck a beautiful three-foot mask that had been hanging from above. I had selected it as a souvenir from my journey to Africa. It lifted off of its hook and hit the ground. The intricate carving shattered into a couple of dozen pieces. I was stunned.

As I began picking up pieces of the mask, I heard the words, "Shatter the masks. It is time to remove all of yours." I looked around the room, because it sounded as if someone had spoken out loud, but I knew the words were coming from inside of me.

My immediate response was, "What in the world? I do not have any masks." I gathered up the rest of the pieces and walked out of the room. As I crossed over the landing, I froze in place. I never realized how many masks I had. There were masks on every wall of my home. It was basically a collection gathered over time. How could I never have noticed it before? I even had pictures of masks. I began walking through different rooms in the house. I found two to three masks in each room, totaling twenty-five in all.

When travelling, I would select things here and there, but had never connected this attraction to masks. Now it seemed as if the objects had actually selected me. I unconsciously bought masks from everywhere.

I knew everything meant something and I was obviously being shown that the masks needed to come down. It was time to become brutally honest with myself so that I could discover where the masks in my life really were.

Endeavoring in new creative choices was not just about answering questions, affirming desires, and implementing action. A new experience of life was directly connected to authentic living. I had to clean up my stuff. I had to get completely into alignment if I wanted my life, my vision, and manifestation to line up with me. I had to identify who I was being that was really not my true Self. The first step would be to identify all of the masks I wore. At the very least, there must have been as many faces to me as had been on my walls.

Kaitlin's Story

A young woman, age thirty-eight, walked into my healing center. Kaitlin was seeking coaching around her aggressive nature. She was strong in her mannerisms and had challenges at work with other female figures. She was also holding a lot of anger and it came through in her interactions. Kaitlin was a loner and quite disconnected from her parents emotionally, although she visited them often. As of late, her experiences in life were getting harder and harder. She found herself doing more and more for less and less.

When she first walked in, I noticed the shirt she was wearing. It depicted Rosie the Riveter, the iconic figure symbolizing feminism and woman power. At the same time, she was wearing a very delicate, pink pearl bracelet and stud earrings. It was an odd combination because one was so masculine in energy and one so utterly feminine. She also had her guard up. Although something was pulling her toward coaching, something was also in her stance that said, "I have to hold myself back and stay as I am to be safe." I thought it was interesting that she chose a woman to coach her when her primary issue had been in dealing with women.

We had several sessions together but Kaitlin was having a challenge getting into her emotional body. She held intense antagonism towards other women and that is where she stayed stuck. She could not connect to herself or to anyone else.

Something kept tugging at me, but I could not put my finger on it. A subtle part of her was so very soft, but most of the time she seemed to be wearing a coat of armor. She was portraying one thing on the surface, but I could feel something entirely different wanted to express from her. I asked if we could meet at her home for the next session. I needed to see her environment so that I could determine what was really going on. I knew there would be symbolism that would help me shift things emotionally so that she could break through. She agreed.

The moment I walked into her home, I got it. It was completely out in the open, but yet so hidden from the rest of the world. The home was very feminine and soft, beautifully decorated with flowers and lush fabrics. Above the fireplace was a print of four women huddled together like sisters. There were statues of women as well, strong and regal, but intensely feminine. In the bathroom was a sculpture of two women, one behind the other. The bedroom had a large mask and costume of a geisha. I could see what was going on.

We sat down to begin our coaching session. She wanted to lead with an issue at work, involving another woman she was in conflict with. As we worked with that, she became more and more agitated. I asked her to close her eyes for a series of questions. I started off with a couple of general questions so she would sink into a more comfortable place and more naturally speak her truth. I asked a couple of questions regarding relationships with men. Her reply was, "They are great. They're like buddies. I have dated quite a few but nothing serious developed. I am just not interested in a committed relationship."

She had not had a long-term romantic partner, but did go on casual dates now and then. She claimed to like alone time. I had been building up to a few specific questions.

"Kaitlin, I want you to breathe deeply. Allow the first answer that comes to mind." I gave her a minute to relax deeply. 'Would you be interested in dating any of the women at work?'

Kaitlin immediately stopped breathing.

"Kaitlin, breathe." As she began to breathe again, I asked, "Do you find any of the women at work attractive."

Again her breath stopped high in the chest. It was the perfect fight or flight response.

"Deep breath . . . good. First answer what comes to mind: Would you like to date any of the women at work? Would you like to date a woman?"

Kaitlin immediately burst into tears. In an instant, her rigid posture softened and a different side of her started to reveal itself. In the softest whisper, she replied. "Yes."

Here was the mask. Kaitlin had a preference for women that she had denied her whole life. Her whisper illustrated self-judgment and shame. Because of that, she intentionally created conflict with women to keep them away. This way she would not have to face or act on her natural impulses.

She looked up at me, with tears streaming down her face. "How did you know? I did not even know."

I pointed to the picture above the fireplace and mentioned how loving it appeared. She revealed that the name of it was "Loving." The bathroom statue, again two women standing very close, one having the other's back. Finally, the geisha, a symbol of traditional values, yet one who wears a mask to play the role of wanting intimacy and the favor of men. The elements of the space such as flowers and soft fabrics illustrated a desire for the feminine nature to be out and flowering.

I also explained that the thought arose the first day she came. I had needed confirmation. Her shirt was very masculine in nature, although a female was depicted. It is who she felt she had to be in the world. Her jewelry, pink pearls, symbolized something desiring to be seen and expressed behind the hard shell. The pink of the pearls related to love and self-love. The messages had been all around her but she would not see them.

She could not be emotionally connected to her parents, out of fear of their judgment. She could not emotionally connect with the natural attraction to women because of the shame and judgment she internalized from her family's views on gay couples. Kaitlin's anger was really toward herself for not following her natural desires. She projected the animosity outward, so there would be no one available to fill those needs. Antagonism was a way of pushing other women away.

Over time, Kaitlin worked through the shame and self-doubt. She also healed relationships at work because her approach with others was dramatically changed just from the awareness she had gained. As Kaitlin allowed herself to be who she was naturally, her whole life transformed. She was no longer introverted, never had issues with women again, and was at peace. She also allowed that soft side that displayed itself in her surroundings to be her new identity. Her fight had not been with other women; it had been with herself. All she needed to allow was Love and "Loving." Kaitlin only needed to stop denying her own feminine essence and expression.

Song: Musical of the Soul

I have always loved music because of its ability to facilitate a connection to the heart and soul. It is healing and moving. Driving down the highway one day, I began thinking about where all music comes from, what its ultimate purpose is, and where it is directed. I surmised that all inspiration comes from the original Creator Source. With this in mind, all songs must have a specific design and clearly state their ultimate purpose.

I began listening deeply to the songs that I resonated with. I realized it was a conversation. These songs were finding me. I was connecting to them because they told me about me, about my life. They resonated with a situation I was experiencing at the time. The songs helped me connect to someone around me. Since people are a projection of the Self, the song would seem directed outward. This was helpful in connecting with the song, inner emotions, and the experience with the other person.

However, if there is no one else in the room but me and God (or whatever name you would call this Higher Power), the song would have to be for me and God. Either God was singing to me, or I was courting God by using a song someone else had channeled from the Great Mind. I decided to try it with every song I could.

I discovered it did not matter what song, this conversation worked. They all could be heard as if between the Creator and the created. Regardless of if it was heavy metal, opera, ballads, pop, or country, every set of lyrics could hold that perspective. It was completely intriguing but not surprising. Artists are inspired by creation. The lyrics would have to connect to the Source of that. From that viewpoint, every song is a hymn, a prayer, a ballad . . . a Love song. They are all dialogues that resonate and intertwine between masculine and feminine, heart and soul, Lover and Beloved.

I knew it must go deeper. If God, Source Energy, flows in, as, and through all of its creation, then it flows through me. This would mean all the songs I resonate with must be about me, speaking to me, in uniting that which flows in, as, and through me. I began wondering if songs were inspired as a form of guidance. What if they are illustrating a journey piece by piece? What if a collection of songs that truly touched an individual somehow string together bits of the "game of life"? Would they show me the story I had been living and was to live? When I looked back, my experiences have shown they do tell a story. I had my own life soundtrack. In fact each period of my life seemed to have one.

I love the way that each of our lives depicts as a Broadway performance. Have you ever made a playlist of the songs that were your favorites growing up during a specific period of life, even now? It is amazing how they will tell your story. These are songs that resonate deeply. They are your tunes, your rhythm of life playing itself out. They open the heart and speak of your soul, beckoning you to connect. These are the dots connecting.

When embarking on a new experience, have you had the synchronistic experience of hearing songs that are speaking your heart and mind? This is your Broadway musical beginning a new show. It is your very own version of *Grease, Les Miserables,* or *The Sound of Music.* It is the journey of the soul played out in its heights of bliss, sadness, love, tragedy, and triumph. Through the hearts, souls, and gifts of others, you'll recognize someone else knows your story, because they are singing the words. They are you and you are they . . . we are all One.

Create your "experience" playlists. Every year, create your own album version of YOU. You will begin to see the interweaving of this amazing musical rendition of your soul journey. As a sound diary of your life, this commemorates the celebration that you are. You will discover how easily you step into yourself when you listen. And in those moments you forget who you are, who you have been, and why you are taking some of the courageous steps you are choosing. The lyrics will remind you.

They are the voice of the wounded you, the orphaned inner child, the courageous one, and the Higher Self. You were taught that feelings of sadness, anger, pain, and disappointment are wrong, bad, or dishonorable. You have been told to get rid of them, to change and get over those feelings. I say not. They are good and honorable. They are part of your celebration of becoming. They are the beginning of the path back home. Bring them back home into the body. Celebrate all of that—play your music! Acknowledge them for what they have taught you. Appreciate them for what they have allowed you to see. Honor them for the lessons they have helped you learn. Cherish them for how they have helped you make new choices. Love into all of it for breaking your heart open so you could have the opportunity to know who you really are. Embrace it so that you may become whole again.

Songs get you into your body. They make you move the body. They are a fun way to energize and stay in the emotional body as well. This exercise will assist the process of processing. When you engage in the feeling of where you are in the moment, rather than suppressing emotions, numbing, or hiding them, you facilitate creation-birthing a higher version of the moment. Integration and relationship with the Self assist in creating greater manifestation and expansion through sound. Be with it. Dance to it. Sing along. Catch your rhythm. It is all attempting to have you "note" who you.

A song may pull you deeper into experiences of bliss. It may ask you to wallow in the depths of your pain. It could ask you to believe in more than you have let yourself have. These rhythms help you wash through the stories that have gotten stuck in your being. The song assists you in affirming and creating a new future that is already resting within the field of infinite possibility. It is feeling that manifests creation; let songs take you to feeling.

If standing in an experience of pain, let music get you deeper into the pain so that the heart opens. When the space opens, you feel so you can heal. For emotion stuck in the body to release, we have to move our bodies, feel the energy, and allow it to dance in the spirit for a while so it is seen. This acknowledgment helps the pain pass through so that you can make choices and allow changes. You are asking on some level to do this or you would not attract these sound streams of your Self to you. An infinite array of streams constantly burst forth for the knowing of Self. Some make way to you, others are waiting for you to rise up and meet them.

Carol's Story

Carol was a young woman working through many life transitions at once. Having held herself back for so many years, it appeared everything in her world was coming to a close. A serious ten-year relationship was ending. She was released from her job. Her home had gone into foreclosure. She was experiencing lower back issues and kidney stones. She perceived life as caving in but steadfastly held a positive frame of mind. I saw it all as something new trying to birth, but there was some incongruence going on.

Her desire was to be more authentic, living a life of balance. She wanted to feel secure instead of feeling like the bottom would drop out from under her at any minute. Her actions were not matching up with the dysfunction. It appeared that she was working toward positive change, but there was an undercurrent of creating self-sabotage.

Although all of our issues arise from early childhood wounds, Carol refused to discuss the past. She insisted that her childhood was very happy and there was nothing to look at. That left me only the space of what the current experience was trying to show her. Perhaps in uncovering that, I could get her to look into the past as well.

I felt as though she were hiding something that was going on in the current experience. Some of her self-created life boulders did not add up. As an assignment, I asked her to take an overview of the last year and compile a playlist of songs she had downloaded. I knew these would be things that had touched her in some way. She questioned the exercise, but I told her to trust it.

A couple of weeks later she brought in her music player and I began listening to the songs. They told me her story. The songs were a mix. They consisted of letting go, heartbreak, and pain, but there were also songs of flirtation, invitation, and courtship. There were themes directly opposing each other in the mix. Certain songs held the energy of loss and grief while the others were joyful and soaked in new love. It was apparent that although she was at a time of a loss of letting go of the long-term relationship, she had left it quite a while before. I suspected she had had another love interest for at least a year. If the signs were correct, the shame and guilt of having an affair were creating the backlash of experiences that had been unexplainable in her life. Then some real transformation could occur.

I asked her to close her eyes and proceeded into a guided meditation. I used her music. I began with some of the songs of breaking up and I could see the sadness in her face and body language. Her hands were closed as fists and her lips were pursed. After a couple of these, one of the love songs came on. Immediately her body changed. A small smile, trying to hide, began spreading across her face. Her hands opened upon her lap.

"Good, you look as if you are beginning to relax. What are you feeling?"

"Release. Love. Happiness."

"Where is it in your body?"

"I feel it in my heart and in my lower belly." (Sacral chakra: relationship center, deeply nourishing). In saying that, she adjusted herself as if she had experienced some pain in the lower back.

"There is something specific that helps you feel this way. I want you to imagine the person or object that brings about this feeling. See them right in front of you. Really see them and deepen your feeling of love.

Now notice something is rising up within you and it is sitting in your lower back. It is something you want to say to this person or object of affection."

Immediately the smile waned and her jaw tensed. Her hands went to the front of her lower gut as if in protection. Her left hand curled back into a fist with the other draped over it for protection. She sat silently.

"What is it you feel the need to protect, Carol? Speak it? What does your lower back desire to say?"

With a bit of hoarseness and a slight cough, "Why can't you choose me? Why can't you love me the way I love you? Why can't you value me?" Her words held heat as her right hand gripped her left a little stronger.

"Carol, who are you talking to? I want you to know you are safe. I am here to help you get your power back and have what you truly desire. Trust me. Who has your power?"

"I have been having an affair with a married man for a year and he will not leave his wife. All the while my life is falling apart. I know he loves me but he is not available to back me up." It all blurted out at once as her hands went to her face.

There it was, the source of the back pain. She was not feeling "backed up." The kidney stones were because of the anger in her relationship area of the body, possibly stemming from both relationships. She had unconsciously recreated the same relationship scenario as in the past. Her hands had gone to her stomach to protect herself because she had given away her power.

The foreclosure was showing she was not feeling valued and could not value herself enough to authentically have what she wanted. She had given away her bodily home for nothing in return. This resulted in financial loss because she was at a loss for herself. Her home was releasing her so she could see how she undervalued herself. It was all happening for closure of healing wounds of the past being held in her body home. This was the cauldron of guilt which was contributing to a messy breakup and being fired from her job.

However, the experience of being in love, because she was able to hold the vibration of loving and being loved, also opened the way for new opportunities. Even though the relationship was still dysfunctional, she was able to stay in love much of the time. The codependence of the relationship would pull her back into the old paradigm and like manifestations. If she could authentically have this love or choose to honor herself by being open to a different experience that could love and honor her fully, life would open in an even greater way. Carol was open to this change.

We were able to go back and look at early childhood experiences that contributed to beliefs in abandonment, receiving less than she deserved, and self-value. Carol was finally ready to clean up her life, starting from the beginning, and it would serve her well.

In a few months' time, her primary relationship ended on good terms. Carol cut off the affair she had been having, after realizing he was not planning on leaving his wife. She began a new career. Carol also began taking time for herself, developing a deeper inner connection and outer self-care experience.

One year later, Carol was in a wonderful new relationship, in an authentic way. It was honoring, loving, and joyful. She had ventured into a business of her own and was thriving. Her new expression of self-value, self-care, and self-love was revealing itself in her outer world. Experiences and people appearing externally were now mirroring the newly emerging inner landscape.

Books: Speaking the Write Way

I have always read the right book at the right time. They just end up in my hands. I come across books that call to me and I buy them. Other times, I am given the book I need to read. There have even been times where I bought a book and placed it on the shelf. It would sit there for a while and then, all of a sudden, I would have an inclination to read that particular one. When I follow that guidance, the writer speaks directly to the experience I am in. There have also been times where I begin a book and get to a certain point and stop. No matter how I try, I cannot complete the book. There is incredible resistance. But, at some point later, I am able to resume the book and the remaining information is relevant but would not have been at any other point in my journey. I could not have read it earlier because I would not have gotten it.

Could it be that books choose you as well? It would seem so. Several months before I arrived at the courage and confidence to leave my marriage of eighteen years, a series of books began entering my life. I knew enough to recognize that they were coming to prepare me for something I was yet to begin experiencing. My soul was getting ready to lead and guide me toward enacting major change in my life. These books appeared as book review submissions or personal selections while travelling, but they arrived in a particular order to speak to the next step in my journey. Several Yoga and Chakra healing books arrived in a row, three of each. That was a clear message for health and self-care. These were all exactly what I needed at the time to build strength and focus. They have proven to make the walk gentler. The books came one by one, to support my next best steps for transformation. I knew this to be Source Presence guiding me. All works are really the voice of Creator speaking as and through another to Self.

There is nothing new that needs be written but there are many voices that need be heard. Each voice of the Greater Self speaks to certain aspects of the smaller selves wandering and waiting to reunite. Books become the guiding force and curriculum for the mind and heart, allowing individuals to move along their self-appointed paths.

A moment does arise, however, where the Self desires to speak and an awareness of being the pages of a great text arises. In that moment, there are inspired words to share, thoughts to impart, and wisdom to be recorded. The willingness to experience and express in that way is the YES to being a witness, a teacher, and a minister of one's own experiencing. That YES will also be the voice, healing, and activation in others who also need to receive it in that way. Be willing to be the text; experience being the teacher. Be the experiencing of textbook creation. And experience the reading of all your experience as a wisdom way-shower.

Simran's Textbook Discussion

My life was drastically changing. I felt as if I needed to make changes. I knew the magazine was complete in its mission and really was supposed to have ended December 2011. I had not listened this time. So new themes downloaded as usual, making me feel safe: Jan/Feb—Raising Our Voices, Mar/April—Into the Ashes, May/June—Shedding Our Skins, July/August—Untie the Strong. The issue themes were always given to me and then articles and interviews appeared that were completely in line. It was very magical, synchronistic in fact. Looking back, the magazine had been a journey of the soul curriculum, fully guided and conversational. While it was healing me, it was teaching others. Each issue led exactly where the soul needed to go to shed layers of illusion. The titles said a great deal, but the material provided the space for healing. The individual that came forward to read, engage, participate, and grow brought the sacred aspect.

Following is a chart that gives information about the magazine issues. What I came to realize in the course of the creations is that each issue spoke to exactly where I was by the time it was printed. By the end, it was a full-fledged curriculum of healing and knowing the self.

THE WISDOM OF INSPIRED WRITING: *11:11 MAGAZINE***

	Jan/Feb	Mar/Apr	May/June	July/Aug	Sept/Oct	Nov/Dec
2008	Return to Innocence	Strength, Longevity & Grace	Journey of Hope	Let Freedom Ring	Elements of Our Nature	Oneness
2009	Saying YES!	Being Authentic	Giving & Receiving	A Voice is Calling	Standing in the Gap	An Open Heart
2010	Guiding Light	Break Through	Creating in Confidence	Power Versus Force	On Solid Ground	Changing Paradigms
2011	Lifting Veils	Stepping Into Synchronicity	Conscious Business	Collaborating in Community	Infinite Possibilities	Self-Care Artisan
2012	Raising Our Voices	Shedding Our Skins	Into the Ashes	Untie the Strong	_____	_____

**11:11 Magazine* and all archives are freely accessible as a gift to humanity from Simran at www.1111mag.com or www.simran-singh.com. Click FREE Banner for online access. For additional teachings and support, register for Simran's Free Newsletter on either website.

The path back to wholeness requires a return to innocence, appreciating and acknowledging the strength, longevity, and grace with which one has already lived. In doing so, it becomes a journey of hope where freedom may ring. As all of the elements of individual nature come together, denying none, oneness comes into vision. That oneness integrates more fully by the degree of "YES!" activated. It requires being authentic to and for the Self. In giving and receiving of the Self, a voice begins calling from deep within. We need only stand in the gap for greatness to emerge.

In the meantime, devotion to inner work prepares the heart for opening so that it serves as a guiding light. Breaking through and creating in confidence ushers forth a new life, using power versus force. On the path, the Self finds solid ground, changing the paradigms of life, lifting veils and stepping into synchronicity. An individual can become conscious about the business of Self, collaborate more fully in community, and passionately venture into infinite possibilities. The last rung of waking occurs by becoming a self-care artisan. In honoring the voice of Self as a Light in the world, raising the many voices within, shedding layers of old skin, and placing into the ashes what needs to be burned away, the strong untie themselves. Untying the strong Self begins the path of an awakened journey of the soul.

I was left at the end with an incredible feeling of connection. I was also in deep understanding that my life, as service-oriented and responsible as it had been, had not been authentic in regard to the vastness or divinity my soul desired to express. I knew there was more I was here to experience. I felt the need to unplug for a period and chose to steer clear of all technology for three months. Going on an eleven-day silent retreat in the sacred mountains of Machu Picchu, I engaged deeply with the Universe. This experiencing led to ceasing the magazine as its curriculum was complete (but maintaining the site so it could continue to be accessed), leaving my marriage, and moving across the country with my two children. This was a little bit of a boulder to swallow. Needless to say, a new curriculum began finding me in preparation for the next step, a collection of books, one by one, specifically designed for this part of the path.

Each book appeared in my experience as I became aware of new insights. They served to confirm my intuitions and urge me forward in the directions of my longings of greater conversation with the Universe. This manner of language, through books appearing, is true for all of us. The following are some examples of the books along the way, followed by a paragraph from the book that was meaningful to me. I have followed each one with insights I had journaled prior to reading the book to illustrate how what we need as confirmation or further insight always appears to us. The Universe is always engaging playfully in this way.

Earthing by Ober, Sinatra, and Zucker

"Beneath the feet outdoors is not merely a patch of grass, dirt, sand or concrete. It is an omnipresent source of natural healing energy. WE are electrical creatures on an electrical planet. Nature can support and heal sickness, pain and inflammation. Connect to the earth . . . balance in the earth. Breathe up and through the earth."

A deep part of me had been sensing for a long time that we were not just beings on planet Earth, but an integral part of the Earth. Gaia and humans served each other as conducers and mirrors. Our role was not to feed upon this Mother Earth but to be fed by the connection to her. Gaia, this great Mother, was not here to be a space for us to inhabit, but to be the greater body of us, and we human beings encompass a great part of the neural network connection.

Courage by Debbie Ford

"Every day we are confronted with hundreds of choices that either make us feel confident and strong or rob us of the things we desire most. When understanding how to be confident, stand in strength, and feel good about the self, a new self emerges with the power to accomplish anything."

I realized the further I travelled down the rabbit hole of my own understanding, the farther I ventured from traditional thought. I was being asked to make a choice between what had always been the norm and the new conversations that were rising up. I was being asked to step into a place of power and confidence, regardless of whether or not anyone would stand along side of me. If I ignored this calling, I would again return to a life of the walking dead. I knew I could not go back, only forward . . .

Beauty Blueprint by Michelle Phillips

"Reclaiming the essence of what makes a person beautiful from the inside out. This is the connection between your outer appearance and deep inner self. Looking good is a byproduct of feeling great."

Once I decided to trust myself and stand strong in the messages and guidance that the Universe was illustrating through my experience, I began tapping into a beauty that I had long forgotten. A place of innocence and freedom had been waiting inside. In choosing to walk the road less travelled, I found the essence that had disappeared long ago. The mere glimpse of that kind of power and vulnerability within myself gave me the ability to see myself in a whole new way, inside and out.

When Things Fall Apart by Pema Chodron

"There is only one approach to suffering that is of long lasting benefit. That involves moving towards painful situations with friendliness and curiosity, relaxing into the essential groundlessness of the entire situation. In the midst of chaos, the truth and love that is indestructible reveals."

These places of courage and innocence that I was gaining the confidence to step into allowed me to make choices in my own life that I had long feared making. I was finally ready to truly let my life fall apart, but with an openness, and a willingness. I did not see it as endings. These walls that were crashing all around me were, in fact, new beginnings. As the façade of the life I had created crumbled away, only that which was real remained. Those pieces of truth, love, authenticity, and curiosity were enough to stand on to build something new.

The Wisdom of No Escape by Pema Chodron

"Say yes to life by making friends with ourselves and the world, and accepting the delightful and painful situation of 'no exit.' It exhorts us to wake up wholeheartedly to everyday life as our primary spiritual teacher and guide."

I now knew I am not here to live life. I am here to be life . . . to be aliveness. I had always been the doing of life. It was now time to sink into the being of life. All of life was here to teach me and guide me as pieces and parts of me. This required me to love into any and everything that appeared in my experience, otherwise I was saying "no" to loving myself.

Serving Humanity by Alice Bailey

"True service is the spontaneous outflow of a loving heart and an intelligent mind, it is the result of being in the right place and staying there; it is produced by the inevitable inflow of spiritual force and not by strenuous physical plane activity; it is the effect of a man's being what he truly is, a Divine son/daughter of God, and not by the studied effect of his words and deeds."

My insights began flooding me as I realized how separate we all make ourselves from the outside world. In this intense need and fear around taking care of ourselves and having enough, we continually separate ourselves from the rest of who we are. We separate ourselves from the allness that is the truth. In doing so, we create the lack and more fear. In embracing the rest of humanity as the self, the heart can open itself to loving the fullness of self. In doing so, the individual becomes larger and receives life from the rest of itself.

These were speaking into the parts of my experience where I had reached a glass ceiling. They had come in as guidance to lift me beyond my own blocks. Life falling apart is never the issue. How we handle life falling apart is. The crumbling away of the known is necessary to embark on the unknown. The unknown holds adventure, possibility, and YOU. Otherwise there is no growth. Do not view change, falling away, or breakdowns as negatives. These are gifts urging you out of the nest to spread your wings and fly. Regardless of the individual, all are on a journey that requires stretching, growing, learning, and changing. It comes through the experiences of attainment, awareness, acceptance, and release. It is the cycle of birth, death, and rebirth as we reincarnate repeatedly throughout our lives.

Books provide steps toward understanding. They maintain that we are never alone in space or experience. Allow these guiding lights to connect you to a greater experience while preparing, training, inspiring, and grounding you into the next stage of your experiencing.

Review of Language Play: Nouns

Language Play provides an opportunity to create an opening within yourself to integrate your experience fully. Each section will engage you in an inquiry that ultimately supports you in learning the language of the universe. This is not work. It is play, intended to be engaged in with curiosity and adventure. As the book progresses, you will develop the mechanics necessary to more easily have your conversation with the Universe.

Language Play of Nouns is intended to assist you in understanding the conversational structure that your life is using to speak to you. Nothing is random. Everything in your experience is appearing for your highest good. These things are not only here for you, but as you and the overall experience of you.

Angels

- Who have been the living angels that broke you open?
- Who have you been a living angel for?
- Do you ask assistance from the angelic realm?
- Do you let yourself experience the answers?

Dreams

- Journal night dreams, and note the feelings that arise.
- Note the specific people or things that you remember and determine what aspect of you is being revealed.
- Spend time daydreaming. Focus eyes upward upon the third eye. Feel into the heart space. Breathe into the solar plexus.

Art

- Look around your home for illustrations of your life experience.
- Look around your workplace for illustrations of your work experience.
- Notice what you are given as gifts from this point forward.
- Notice what you are drawn to.

Songs

- What are the songs you are drawn to? Make a playlist.
- What are they asking you to feel?
- What does this take you to?
- Where is that in your body?
- Are they asking you to feel, act, love, forgive, acknowledge, or accept?

Books

- What books are coming to you?
- Where are they speaking to within you?
- Are they asking you to move or be still? To feel or to acknowledge?
- Is there a sequence of books that has come forward as a guiding message?

Have Fun . . .
Play . . .
Discover the many versions of you, that are YOU . . .
Who do you think you are not?
You are the ONE.

9

The Verbs

Language requires that action exist for sentences, paragraphs, dialogue, and communication to be formed. The Universe is no different in its instigation of action. Symbols and signs are also showing up to tell you to do something. In being human, there is a fine balance between being and doing. Some are so busy doing that they forget about the being. There are also those that spend so much time being that nothing gets done.

Spiritual beings in a human body possess the opportunity to dance between doing and being, allowing the ebb and flow of life to assist for conscious creation. Less expenditure of effort can be developed, utilizing the power of presence as a guide for when to move and when to be still. Once the deep knowing of presence is cultivated, it can be carried into the actions of doing. One may follow the "verb" messages that illustrate this clearly: names, numbers, and locations.

The reason that numbers, locations, and names are the verbs is because they ask you to sit in that place of stillness first. They are the position of presence from where one must move. Presence in itself is an action. It is the action of being. These illustrations of language help an individual understand the next cycle unfolding and how to move, grow, and be within that through conscious action.

My experiences of numbers are as promptings of action in response to bringing my presence to thoughts. In those moments, I always see guiding numbers. Their meanings request something of me.

The places I have lived begin with a number, which provides the overall purpose and scope of my time there. The name implies a greater degree of action going on in the space, reflecting the action going on within my being. From this point of reference, the actions necessary for conscious inner work and integration reveal easily. Locations are direction. They are clear messages of where you are physically so you may understand emotionally, mentally, and energetically where you are to go. Movement in the world into new and varied locations is a reference to movement in spirit to new and varied locations. You are always in locomotion. You are always in the act of moving from place to place.

10

Numbers

Everything in the Universe boils down to numbers, ultimately a binary code of one and zero. This makes sense to me because I have experienced communication through numbers for a long time. Angels speak through numbers. They have guided me, telling exactly when to follow a path and when not to, providing reassurance when I was in doubt and creating endless synchronicity.

My experiences with 11:11 are simply magical. 11 is a Master number. All double digit numbers are Master numbers: 22, 33, 44, 55, 66, 77, etc. People begin seeing 11 when engaging on a soul or spiritual path. 11:11 is the gateway between physical and spiritual, illusion and reality, mind and heart—a human doing spirituality versus a human being spiritual. As long as you are focused on ritual and methodology as our spirituality, you are doing spirituality. Spirituality cannot be a "doing" or a "trying" because it is the "all" of you. Your engagement with everything as you, and as Divine, is the "being" of spirituality. As individuals are grow awareness of their spirituality, they will begin to see the other double digit numbers and some triple as well: 222, 333, 444, 555, etc. 11:11 will graduate in number and frequency as you continue saying YES to your authentic nature and wholeness.

Whether you see these numbers or not does not matter. You are seeing something repeatedly and that boils down to, "The Universe has your back. The Universe is trying to get your attention and speak to you. Know that you have support always." Whenever numbers appear repeatedly, your question or prayer is being answered. Numbers are one of the easiest methods to begin understanding what the Universe is saying to you.

An easy way to begin is basic numerology. All numbers are added together and brought to a single digit. This number is an overall theme of the experience at hand. The only time it is not brought to a single digit is when it is a Master number. Master numbers have magnified traits. Try it out with your name. Numerology will illustrate your personality, soul path, strengths, and weaknesses based on the letters of your name and the related numerical value for each. There are many books on numerology and some are listed in the resource section.

The Universe communicates number sequences in many ways. Your attention will be gently drawn in a certain direction so that you look up, or turn around, in time to notice the time on a clock, a number on a license plate, a mailbox, or a phone number on a billboard. It will be something you focus on, not just every number that passes your way. The Universe will continue this method of dialogue in greater frequency as you begin following it. Signs will keep appearing for you to take notice of and say, "OK, this is weird! What does this number sequence mean?" For example, you may see 11:11 or 12:12 every time you look at a clock, or perhaps when you're driving past a billboard you are always drawn to look at the 555 that is part of a telephone number. It can also be other random numbers like 74 or 165 or 2. All numbers have a specific meaning. There are books and online sites that interpret the meanings of specific numbers.

Those who are aware of this phenomenon become adept at reading the meaning of number sequences. We are a matrix and everything boils down to numbers in the end. The Universe can provide guidance, advice, and answers to any question you may ask, however important or mundane. For example, you could see 333 when thinking about a new venture or moving to a new city, anything that is being urged from the heart. This number confirms you are being supported in your desires. In dealing with partnerships, you may see the number two or pairs of things, such as birds to indicate if something is positive and guided by spirit. You can ask any question. Do not look for signs or avoid them. They will find you at the right time regardless of your efforts.

The most important element of the numbers you are seeing is not necessarily the number or what it means. The most essential element is the feeling instilled within you. This is a direct illustration that you are being supported. You can place faith that you are being seen, acknowledged, supported, and loved, every time you see one of your common numbers.

THE ACTION MEANING OF NUMBERS

Number	Numerical Traits	Numerical Action to Take
One	New beginnings, strong will, purity, positivity	Start new ventures, physical action, mental action, urgency
Two	Quiet power, tact, kindness, balance	Choose now, exert fairness and proper judgment
Three	Magic, expression, creativity, advantage, intuition	Express creatively, live adventurously
Four	Stability, solidity, calmness, home	Root and center yourself, have persistence and endurance
Five	Travel, adventure, motion	Take action, take a trip, move, radical change
Six	Harmony, balance, sincerity, love, truth	Forgive, create action steps of balance in life
Seven	Education, mystery, imagination	Take actions toward stillness, prayer, meditation
Eight	Success, wealth, reputation, business, cycles	Create systems, establish routines, work toward goals
Nine	Healing, attainment, satisfaction, accomplishment, influence	Use talents and abilities, serve humanity

11

Names

A name given to something is guidance toward the real nature of that place or individual. When something is named, it is being given its destiny, character, traits, and flaws. In a subtle way, it also reveals the weaknesses, challenges, and obstacles that might be encountered.

A name can not only tell you about the personality and characteristics of the person, place, or thing, it will also numerically divulge soul path, destiny, talents, traits, and obstacles.

Your name is a sacred prayer. Each time your name is stated, it reinforces all of the elements that you are. Each time you say your own name, you imprint on the world who you are based on how you feel about yourself. Chanting your name with the intention of self-love will have a completely different effect than chanting your name with self-loathing.

Names depict the soul journey of an individual by illustrating who they really are within the spiritual meaning and significance of the name. The same is the case for how we name anything. Name combinations will reveal greater depth of one's story. Your life and the surrounding components along with your history are a sacred text. You are a walking bible. The individuals that surround you most closely create the full expanse of this great book.

Name: It Is Your Nature

As I looked at family dynamics, I noticed something I had never seen before. How deeply did their presence serve? Did it begin the moment of birth, even in the names given? Did their message move throughout life, expanding when they expanded into relationships and family? I began looking deeper and was astonished at the beauty of the story, of my personal matrix. There were four of us.

My elder brother's name meant "beloved friend." His nickname meant "powerful battler." His wife's name meant "wisdom." My younger brother's name meant "God's feet" and his nickname meant "great hero." His wife's name meant "calm and deliberate actions." My sister's name meant "humility." Her nickname meant "small." Her husband's name meant "who is like God." My mom's name meant "king" and my father's name meant "invincible." The family name meant "battle attack." My own name was "she who hears and repeats God's words" and my nickname meant "to die over." My husband's name meant "victory" or "victorious."

It was interesting to me. A complete storyline lay within the family names. There was an entire plot, characters and script. Each name and nickname illustrated a person's spectrum of wound and greatness. The names, whose goal was to lead them through the journey of transformation, would provide opportunity to reach the fulfillment of their second name.

FAMILY NAMES

	Given Name	*Nickname*	*Spouse Name*
Parents	Battle attack	King (Mother)	Invincible (Father)
Brother	Beloved friend	Powerful battler	Wisdom
Brother	God's feet	Great Hero	Calm and deliberate actions
Sister	Humility	Small	Who is like God
Simran	She who hears	To die over	Victory

The story line was out of this world but then aren't we all if we are of the Divine?

Once upon a time, there was a land where battles raged. These battles were attacks on various levels of people's mental, emotional, physical, spiritual, energetic, and psychic landscapes. The King ruled the land with a firm hand. Yet strong and dark forces of time would seek to overtake them. They would seek to rise above their great opponents. Any obstacle that appeared along the way was the illusion.

They would run from death, feeling that was the end. But no, they had "to die over" their own "smallness" to realize their "invincibility." In overcoming smallness, the King's "beloved friend" became a "powerful battler," defeating the forces that would torture the mind and thereby resulting in great "wisdom." The one who exhibited "God's feet" would move with "calm and deliberate actions" through energetic and psychic fields, ultimately becoming a "great hero." In allowing the "small" to kneel to their physical entanglements, "humility" would reign in the one who is like God. In being willing "to die over" the heart wrenching blockages, cold temperatures, and barren lands, she would hear and repeat the name of the Unified Being on the journey to "victory."

Spiritually this symbolized the story we were to play out to one another. In addition, we each represented the qualities we needed to experience and the ones we needed to grow into. Finally, we were mirrors to each other, illustrating other things we would need to uncover within ourselves.

In continuing down the generations, I noticed the names of grandchildren and great grandchildren continued the story. This was a story of the journey to enlightenment.

I knew this had not been manipulated or orchestrated. These names were not researched before the children were born. All the names were selected in a sacred process of Holy ceremony. The sacred text is opened randomly. Using the first letter of the first word on the left hand side, the search begins for a name beginning with that letter. The hunt begins for a name that everyone likes. It does not matter if a different method is used, a person was adopted, or someone married or divorced. All names represent an aspect of the story.

The names of the older grandchildren, born to "Beloved Friend" and "Wisdom" illustrated this. The eldest meant "victory of the people." The second eldest meant "noble one and bringer of peace or peace of mind." The youngest meant "protector and benefactor of splendor." These children are still part of the shedding of generational systems. However they are illustrating a turn in this particular lineage. The battle would result in a victory of the people where peace of mind is attained, bringing the land protection and splendor.

The younger grandchildren of the other siblings were all names of God. They came in knowing they are pure God beings. They are star or crystal children, born during certain years and having particular gifts and characteristics. There were five of these children supporting a deeper integration of

Divine knowing and meaning of life. They are listed from eldest to youngest so it was very clear to me the progression of consciousness. They were here to not only continue the sacred story, but also experience the story.

Child 1 means Peace Reborn

Child 2 means Dear Beloved

Child 3 means Lotus Flower

Child 4 means God walking

Child 5 means God's Service

Finally, there is the first great grandchild in this scenario. The child's name means "Pure White Light." This was one step farther than the grandchild in the evolution of consciousness. This illustrated the unification of all gods into One presence of Light.

I sat back in awe of what I had become aware of. I checked all the details and the name meanings were accurate. In that moment, I discovered a profound truth. Each and every individual on the planet is a Master and creator of destiny. Our abilities to create were limited by nothing but our own minds and ability to be open to infinite possibility. I had seen it in my own family. Some had reached for their full destiny while others were on their way.

Everything did mean something. There was a pattern and grid that could be followed. These family lineages were all sacred bibles unto themselves, recanting the story of evolution in their own way, not unlike the many stories in various sacred texts around the world. I could see now. It does not matter how you received your name; it has meaning. It is here to tell you your nature. It is a message and guide for you to know that you can reach high into Mastery of that which you represent.

Every human being is a sacred text. Your families and lineages create individual bibles, not to be taken literally but viewed as a grand expanse of the oneness unfolding. You are to discover the metaphor, symbolism, and metaphysics within each story line, chuckling along the way at the magnificent way you embellished your sacred book. God has a sense of humor. God wants you to have fun because God is having fun with you, as you. You are the creation of God Presence and the God of creation within the grand unified field of Divine Presence.

If I could create a complete story of genesis within my own world, I could create anything. This is not to forsake the sacred texts, prophets, or master teachers that have come before, but instead to underscore what they were trying to get across. You wrote your story. You are living it. It is Divine—every moment of it. See it for the grand play that it is.

12

Locations

Where do you live? Where in your world do you call home? Where do you work? What are the places you frequent? What street do you live on? Where do you hang your hat, your heart . . . your soul?

All of the places you reside are essential to bringing you home inside of yourself. They express your unique essence and vibration of where you are in the moment. They reveal what you must do to attain the higher essential version of you. In addition, they hold the energetic imprint of what must be resolved within you.

All places already have a specific vibration. There has been an amazing history all over the planet, and like human beings, places will continually have the same experience until someone or something transmutes the energy. People are attracted to places that hold their unresolved emotional energy. The reason this occurs is for the higher good of all. You are the space as well. As you heal yourself, you heal the space. When you have cleared the energetic imprint within you, a move will occur, taking you to your next best step. Or you will shift the energy, both within you and the space that you can remain in, but have an entirely different experience in the space and of yourself.

There are moments when people who live together will part. This is because two unlike vibrations cannot reside in the same space. The one who leaves does not resonate with the space or the person within the space. In the end, all serves for growth, expansion, unity, and oneness.

Be willing to look at the places you reside beyond being a house, hotel, or workplace. They are extensions of you. They are here to hold you and to be beheld by you. All spaces carry messages of your past and your future. Begin noticing what you feel in a space, not what you think about it.

Oftentimes we will also be prompted as to where geographically we should be. Be cognizant of what seems to continuously pop up for you. You will be led to the area most geographically resonant with your energy. When living in places of resonance, it can be the difference between a life of ease and comfort or challenge and unrest.

It sounds very strange, but all spaces hold energy. They attract you and you attract them for the purpose of mutual healing. There is a method to all things in the Universe. It is a rhythm that moves naturally with its own intelligence. It needs no controlling factor or guidance, as it is perfectly calibrated to be the continuous creation of itself. Energy can only remain energy, however it can transform. As it does, it evolves into a higher level and understanding of itself. Energy grows as we grow. It expands as we expand. It moves when we move.

Rustic Manor

I stood in the empty room reflecting on the many memories that were part of this space, memories charged with spiritual growth and constant choice. It felt good to know that I had changed what was here. I could feel it. This house was cleansed. It seemed like yesterday when I first came to this home. I was brought under the pretense that we were visiting someone, but all of a sudden my husband removed the doormat where a key was hidden and we walked inside.

It was an empty home, like now, but palpably different; a different energy now than there was. At that time I could not sense it. My life had not yet begun to fall apart. I had not attuned my sensitivities. Little did I know that this would be the place that would engage my conscious spiritual journey. I would be broken and broken open. This place would initiate death. It had been charged with the energy of Kali, "beginnings and endings," well before we came here.

In these hallowed spaces, I had grown more than I would have ever dreamed possible. Only here could I have seen beyond the illusions and masks that my world had become. This had been my cave of the dark night and also my sanctuary of peace. I had transformed this property and it had transformed me. I would come to realize that 821 Rustic Manor Court had been symbolic in many ways.

This Master number house was to amplify everything in my life so I would be forced to look within. I thought that my husband had selected the home. Now I realize that the home had selected me. I had work to do and this was the place where I would be challenged enough, in order to perform the mission my soul had determined long ago.

I specifically remember the day of the closing. Everything had gone smoothly and hands were shaken. As we began to rise from the table in the attorney's office, our realtor, who happened to be our old neighbor, placed a large bucket on the desk, "I am going to give this to you. It has all the papers you need in terms of manuals and warranties for items in the house. Take good care of it because I will need it back in six months, when you separate and move out."

I was stunned, to say the least. What an interesting thing to say to someone who has just bought a home. That should have been a clue as to what was to come. "I am sorry. I did not quite understand what you meant. That is an odd thing to say."

"Well now I will tell you the story of the house. No couple has lived in that home very long. They all separate after six months. There have been three separate couples in the home, all ending the same way. The first one built the home. He and his wife had twin girls. The wife ran away with someone, leaving the man and his daughters in the main house. Her parents were living in the guesthouse. The second was a newlywed couple, as was the third. They all ended the same way. So, I will need the box back, intact, if that is the case."

I felt my knees buckle under me. Aside from being a very inappropriate comment, something about it felt very real. There had been something that I felt when I walked into the home. I could not place my finger on it. Now I realized why I felt so sad when I walked through the few times we saw it. I thought I was sad about leaving our other home, which I loved. I was feeling the energy that had been poured over and embedded in the walls, the foundation, the entire structure. I was speechless. We picked up the bucket and went to our new home.

I always had a prayer room in my other living spaces and this would be no different. The first thing I did was pray that the house be blessed and cleared of any past energy. Little did I know I was the clearing agent.

The experiences in the cellular memory of the home would have to detox. The only way to do that was to have the same experience move through us, but find reconciliation and unity rather than separation and divorce.

As time passed, a very different experience of our relationship began to express. I could see changes that I was unable to control. I began to explore energy and spaces more and more. I brought in energy experts and intuitive healers. All of them, without even being told about the history of the house, immediately felt the energy when they walked in. They would place cures and effects to help clear the space. In one instance, a practitioner's tools broke spontaneously. She pulled out another, the same thing happened. Then a third tool broke. She had never experienced that before.

After being silent for several moments, she spoke. "The energy in this home is anchored here and it does not want to go. It will not leave until someone is strong enough to overcome it. You and your husband will have to go through the fire. You may or may not come out. This is a karmic and cosmic energy grid. There is a vortex on this property that has wrapped itself around this energy and keeps magnifying it. There is a lot of sadness and anger embedded in this home and the energies feed on creating more. This energy has been here a long time."

I finally understood. There had been so many changes in the behaviors within the house. My husband had become a completely different man. I could see that things were not right but no one else seemed to. Turmoil increased. As I went from place to place in search of answers and understanding of what was happening to my life . . . what was happening with my husband, I gained access to amazing teachings and practitioners. The more assistance I received, the more I seemed to need, as things became progressively worse. Living in the home was tearing me apart. Now I realize it was breaking me open.

Then it happened, six months later, my husband wanted to leave. I could not believe it. It made no sense! Life had changed so drastically, he had changed so dramatically. How could a home alter people and life to this degree? I convinced him to stay but it continued. Every six months the cycle repeated and I found myself in tears, asking what I needed to do differently for him to stay. Who did I need to become? What could I do to make him happy? Every time I diffused the situation and tried to make life peaceful, it would settle for a while, only to erupt again a few months later. In the process, I was losing myself. I was losing who I knew myself to be, changing into a numb robot that was trying to do everything right to feel safe in a place that felt so carnivorous.

Seven years later, I could hold him back no longer. The endless six-month cycle had to end. I had done enough reading, work, introspection, and study of energy. I knew I had to surrender. My husband left. He was angry. The energy within the home had consumed him. I remember the day he left. It was almost as if the house took a sigh, as if it had won. I felt as if it was smiling . . . and I had been left there.

I put the house up for sale but no one was interested. I knew I had to change the energy of this place for my son and me if it ever did sell, I would not allow another family to experience what we had.

I began to pray constantly. I built a labyrinth in the front yard. I created water features inside and out for the movement of energy and cleansing. I constantly played high frequency music and placed flowers all over the house. I made sure everything in the home was uplifting and felt good. I could feel things shifting. However, I knew it also required my inner work. Any emotion I held that was low in vibration, denser energies would feed on.

Oftentimes, I would host practitioners at the Believe Center whom I knew to be highly skilled. On one particular occasion, a practitioner asked me if I was aware of the dark-haired woman in the house. She had kept him up all night. "She is very angry with you. She believes you have her son and wants you to leave here."

I knew whom he was speaking of. I had just recently seen her on the upstairs landing. She appeared as a shadow out of the corner of my eye. But I had known about her a year after we had moved in.

My son was two years old at the time and could speak only a few words. We were sitting in the great room. All of a sudden, in a very clear voice, he turned and said, "Mommy, you go now. My other mommy is here." I sat stunned as I watched my child stop playing and look at me in a very serious manner, with wisdom far beyond his years.

"Where is she honey? What does she look like?"

Not moving his gaze from me, he spoke softly. "There . . . in the garden. See her?" I could not see her, but I knew better than to deny him the vision. "Let her know I am not ready to go yet. She is welcome to stay, but I still want to be your mommy."

He looked toward the garden and then turned back to his toys as if the incident never happened. Then, almost a year later, it happened again while I was tucking him into bed.

He turned and looked at me with the same seriousness. "Mommy, I told you time to go now. My other mommy is here. It is her turn."

"Where is she honey?"

"There. Standing on the water in the white dress. See her?"

"Well, I am not going anywhere. You are my son in this lifetime and I am going to spend every second I can with you. Let her know I will not leave because I love you too much." He never spoke of her again.

I finished relaying the story to the practitioner. After a moment he said, "Yes. She truly believes this is her son. Sage looks like her son. She is Native American. This land and her home were taken from her. She watched as her husband was killed. Her son was carried off. She does not realize she was killed at that time. She has been reliving the trauma and abandonment over and over again."

It clicked! Abandonment was the feeling of sadness I had always felt in this home. This energy was ancient and had not been created by the families who lived within this home before us, but it had played a role in their demise. "Would you come down into the basement and tell me what you hear or experience."

The moment we opened the door to the basement, he jerked back. "Oh my God! The anger! The hatred!" He doubled over and clutched his stomach, as if going to be sick. After steadying himself, we walked downstairs.

I knew something had been down there or had occurred because the air always felt heavy. My son, who was very intuitive, refused to go down there. As we stood in the basement, I could see the practitioner dialoguing with the energy that lived in the space. After he was finished, he motioned for us both to go upstairs.

"There is a lot of pain there, tremendous pain. There is a very large energy, that of an African male. He was a slave. He wants revenge and is extremely angry. He had to watch the murder of his children, the raping of his wife, and then was beaten to death himself. He is reliving those moments over and over because he does not realize he is dead. He does not know they have passed into the Light and are at peace, waiting for him. He is caught in a loop of perception. The same is true for the Native American woman. She does not realize she is dead and that her loved ones are waiting for her in the Light. These souls are in tremendous pain and they are anchoring this pain-filled energy on this property.

"You must pray for them. Send them love and Light. Dialogue with them and help them to understand that their loved ones are fine and they can return to them. It is partially why you were led to this home. You are an open person. You have an open heart, a loving and forgiving heart and a strong spirit. You are one of the rare ones that would be willing to explore and heal this place of its dis-ease. Most people would run away in fear. Their Higher Selves knew this and pulled you here. Your Higher selves negotiated this as your life contracts were being drawn. These are soul mates in spirit form.

"This home also will create the scenarios you and your husband must face. You have a lot of past karma together. In this lifetime, in this home, you both came to bring it to completion. You are to experience a lot of intensity that you have to heal through. In doing so, you will help this space detox its dis-ease. This home is the perfect cauldron to produce that."

This is why the home chose me. I committed to sending love to these two tortured souls. I meditated, calling their families in the hopes of creating a scenario in which they could move on from their earthly prison. I realized that much of the earth must hold a lot of pain, especially in certain areas of historic oppression, which could mean any and everywhere on the planet. No wonder the earth's problems continually progressed. Pain was building blocks of pain, layers upon layers.

In the meantime, I did my own work. My inner landscape needed tending for my outer landscape to once again be fertile, supple, and productive. I had to cleanse my vessel of any anger, sadness, disappointment, shame, regret, or fear. This place had to vibrate in some way with me for me to be here. I had done enough work to know that and was not too arrogant to acknowledge what I might not know about myself. I knew this was why *11:11 Magazine* came through me.

There may have been heavy energy in the home but I had my own arsenal of Light. I knew I had angels, guardians, and guides supporting me. The Universe was supporting me. Everything I needed to heal the space or myself would be brought to me. The further along I got in the creation and curriculum of *11:11 Magazine*, the less dense the atmosphere felt.

I could tell the moment both souls transitioned. The space, all of a sudden, felt very light. Flowers began blooming where they never did before. There were constantly birds, butterflies, and dragonflies in the yard. Deer crossed through the property, which I knew symbolized hearth and home.

The house address speaks its meaning. 821 is an 11 number, the Master number for the gateway of change, the doorway between perception and possibility, illusion and reality, dark and light, positive and negative. "Rustic" represents the old, the embedded thoughts and emotional forms that needed to be cleared—that which is raw and wild and untamed. "Manor" was the home, the mansion, the vehicle that houses all. In the South, "manor" might sound like "mana," which is the sacred, supernatural force that dwells within. This Manor was to represent the aspects of Light and Dark for reconciliation, unification, and completion, so all could be brought home. It was the fine line between separation and connection. Mana also reflects the supernatural force that resides within each of us. "Court" represented a choice between two possibilities. The past three couples chose to go to court. My husband and I decided to court and renew a bond that has since become a stronger relationship and a spiritual union. Everything means something.

Review of Language Play: Verbs

Language Play supports opening yourself to integration of your experience. These inquiries assist you in learning your language with the universe. This is not work. It is play, to be engaged in with curiosity and adventure. You will develop the mechanics necessary to more easily have your conversation with the Universe.

Language Play of Verbs brings an understanding the action within the conversational structure that your life is using to speak to you. Nothing is random. Everything in your experience is appearing for your highest good. These things are not only here for you, but as you and the overall experience of you.

Numbers

- What are the numbers you see repeatedly?
- Do a numerology charting or have a numerology reading performed.
- Notice how numbers appear in relation to various life experiences.

Names

- Get to know the meaning of your name.
- What do the names of other significant people in your life tell you about you?
- What are names you have always loved and what do they mean?
- What is the numerological meaning of your name?

Location

- List the places you have lived.
- What did their addresses represent?
- What specific life events occurred while living in those places?
- What feelings and growth were you meant to tap into?
- Looking back, how did the location initial give you the language that these changes would occur?

13

The Adjectives

The adjectives of the soul conversation provide the descriptors for your experience. They describe in colorful, expressive ways all of the expressions of you. The purpose of the adjectives is to get you in touch with the feeling that you are, the feeling that is embedded within you but unnoticed.

In designing your Godburst experience, you were brilliant in giving yourself additional home spaces that would surround you. Just as you have numerous energetic bodies extending beyond the physical structure, you also have several physical bodies extending beyond your human form. They all relate and will sometimes reflect the same issues at the same time. If this happens, you must really pay attention as something is eminent in your experience.

The awareness I desire for you to take in is that all experiences occur for the sake of unification. You are always being brought back to the unhealed parts of yourself. This is so you can make whole that which, in illusion, appears fragmented. The body, home, and vehicle are the most intimate reflections of your mental and emotional bodies.

As fragmentation occurs, it is held within the energetic fields surrounding you. These energetic bodies consist of etheric, auric, mental, and emotional bodies, extending up to twenty feet beyond your physical human form. Your physical body is not impacted with dis-ease until it has moved through these spheres.

However, if you are holding these spheres out as wide as twenty feet and not dealing with the things clogging the energetic bodies, there will be a reflection in the spaces that rest within that twenty feet. The spaces you frequent that rest in that footage would be your home and your car. This is why they are so intimately linked to your experiences. They are YOU. They hold your energetic imprint from the outside in. They rest within the field of your emotional and mental landscape on a continual basis. You may want to ignore what is suppressed within you, but they will not. They are not attached to them, they are attached to you. Enjoy the exciting collaboration between your body, home, and automobile.

14

The Human Body

The physical human form is the most direct route back into the illusion. It is the spacesuit, in fact the spaceship. Every piece is intimately connected to the Mother/Father Ship. Your physical human form already knows the language of the Universe. It is here to help illustrate for you. But you must look, listen, and feel to decode its dialect.

When you chose your physical vessel, you created every possible resource to assist you in navigating the illusion. But you also chose every resource to discover truth. Dis-ease, sickness, genetic weakness, and discomfort are the fail-safe equipment that has been incorporated as signal mechanisms. These devices—your body systems, organs, blood, bone, tissues, and cells—sound alarms when turning the corner is necessary. These alarms, big or small, will serve to bring you into stillness, questioning, introspection, and alignment if you are willing to connect with yourself and properly service your vehicle's various components. Your body is speaking to you. It is your GPS: Guiding Physical System. It is also trying to help you reestablish communication with the Mother/Father Ship because you have dramatically gone off course.

Within any health issue, great or small, is a message to change direction and chart a new course. The direction is inward. Discomfort is not a force to pull a person out of life experience, but to assist them in moving deeper into their degree of life experiencing. For those truly desiring to learn their native language, delve deeply into what the specific components represent and speak forth. The level of discernment involves the choice between having a passing glance, a surface conversation, or a deeply intimate dialogue. The deeper you dive, the greater the connection and distance of the mission. In this way, one can travel the entire Universe and back, seeing all of the beautiful horizons, instead of staying lost in the parking garage with a stalled vehicle.

Mind you, the deeper exploration of the self and the language of the Universe do not always mean that dis-ease will disappear or heal in the human sense. Sometimes the healing, the very message, is in playing out the dis-ease to full completion. It may even play out as the death of certain human beings in other ways, natural, tragic, or horrific. These souls have chosen to become part of the language itself. They are in oneness to a greater cause, being a catalyst for emotional and energetic transformation. These souls spur additional medical and scientific research. They act as paddles to the hearts of those "walking dead" by shocking them back into life, compassion, and feeling. They are the symbol of the ongoing process of death and life. They are the language of the soul calling all souls home via their reflection. In the name of Love, they say, "I will allow my own journey to be the linguistic example that can rescue and heal a multitude of others." Discomfort supports you reawakening to your senses. The senses are another level of understanding the language being spoken and a step closer to the inner landscape. Just as earth is school, there is opportunity to graduate to different levels of understanding.

Learning to trust the sensing devices of the body is a form of integration for mind, body, and spirit. It brings the language revealing itself on the outside to the core of the spaceship, the point where the soul rests and waits for your awakening. In not only allowing the symbol to reveal its message but also becoming one with it, integration occurs. By discovering the senses and tapping into the texture, scent, color, and feel of what is occurring, the experience deepens, bringing a greater knowing of synchronicity and unfolding dialogue. In order to access the many unseen colors, textures, scents, flavors, and sounds that are available to us, we must first acknowledge, appreciate, and engage with those that reveal themselves on the earthly plane. It is why you manifested a spacesuit, your spaceship. This vehicle is sensory and assists you in having an experiential curriculum. Within experience is the integration and deepening understanding of your soul truth and ultimate conversation the Universe is having with you.

Do not discount a breeze upon your skin, the blue of a jay passing your sight, or the scent of jasmine wafting by. Each is symbolic. Each is speaking to your body, asking to be heard through a specific sense. Every amazing occurrence sits in your body somewhere as a feeling.

These sensory experiences are asking you to disappear into an experience as you did as a child, looking out the window and diving into the possibility of imagination. Let yourself remember. Let yourself discover your unfolding possibility and truth through the gentle words and expanding sentences being spoken.

Issues work themselves from the outside in. Your physical body is the last layer that manifests messages. Aura is life. It is the energy that animates our physical body. The auric field exists in different layers sometimes referred to as harmonics because of the color fields they emit. Each layer of the auric field is a body just as real and alive as the physical body. Each layer is a mini world with its own sense of purpose. The magic of the auric field is in how these mini worlds intertwine and dance with one another. These layers interconnect with one another determining the experiencing of our physical reality.

Maggie's Story

Maggie is an accountant that handles divorce settlements. She had been to multiple doctors for various health issues that arose. Doctors could provide no relief and no advice. Her right big toe had lost movement. In addition, a large swelling developed on her right shin muscle.

I explained to her that the right side of the body was the masculine side of the body. I asked her to reflect on what was happening in her life regarding a male figure or a female figure with a masculine nature. This individual will be the reincarnation of an earlier issue related to her father. This experience occurred to help her identify a deeper issue. I asked her to tap into her emotions and feel in the situation.

I explained, "The feet have to do with trust. The big toe is ego and swelling of the muscle is anger. Your spirit wants you to trust yourself or the situation. Feel the anger and know that it's okay for you to have an ego to express that. It could also mean another's ego is holding you down or back, but nonetheless, you do have anger. These are your instructions:

- Sit and feel the anger or upset. Focus on your shin and big toe. With deep inhales, exhale imagining you are moving the energy that is stuck. Breathe out of your feet. Stand barefoot in the yard, breathing until you feel release.

- In stillness, with the person in mind, have a dialogue to hear what your spirit needs to say.

- Forgive yourself and the other for having created the issue and the health problems.

- In stillness, remember the earliest time you felt the same way with parent or caregiver. Repeat first three steps."

QUICK REFERENCE CHART FOR THE BODY

Chakra	Related Areas	I AM Statement	Experience to Experiencing
Left Side	Feminine Influences	I AM Loved	Giving to Receiving
Right Side	Masculine Influences	I AM Love	Being to Doing, Stillness to Action
Root	Feet to Base of Spine	I AM Trust	Insecurity to Security Separate to Connected
Sacral	Genitals to 2" Below Navel	I AM Creation	Stagnancy to Movement Doubt to Creativity
Solar Plexus	2" Below Navel to 2" Above Navel	I AM Energy	Force to Power Withhold to Willful
Heart	Heart and Chest cavity	I AM Wisdom	Reaction to Response Martyr to Service
Throat	Neck, Jaw, and Shoulders	I Am Truth	Codependent to Independent, Conditional to Unconditional
Third Eye	Mid-nose to High Forehead	I AM Divine	Confusion to Clarity Believing to Seeing
Crown	High Forehead Up	I AM That I AM	Human Being to Spirit Essence

15

The Home Body

Your home is literally an extension of you. Each room, floor, and arising issue is a part of you. These are representations of various levels within you, parts of your life, and internal landscape. Everything symbolizes something. It will communicate with you by allowing certain situations that need tending to arise.

If there are issues at the base level of operation in your life, you will experience foundation issues. If it is action-oriented, the main body of the home will be affected. The problems stemming from mind, mindset, beliefs, and thought forms will illustrate as issues in the roof and attic spaces. Anything to do with plumbing will reference emotional issues. A home is your home outside of your body home. It is the next closest thing to you. The messages will arise in your home before they begin hitting your physical body.

The home body is one of the physical bodies outside the human body which experience uses to navigate and illustrate blockages. The issues we carry will manifest because you are always "in Love." The essence that you are loves you enough to send you messages ahead of time. Your home is you, outside of you.

If you ignore the messages, you will move closer to you by moving through all the things that are you in the world. For example, it will move through your workplace, your car, your home, your furniture, your household items, your clothes until it ultimately hits your body. And if you look back, you will see it too has a pattern. It will manifest in the same areas in each place.

For example, when I am about to experience a large transformation, the ceiling will leak. If I have gotten out of balance working too much, ants will appear.

There is a certain language that you will be able to discern from your home. Why? It knows you, breathes with you, and feels your energy. It has your energy and expresses the blocks within that energy to assist you. Your home will help focus you on what needs personal healing next.

SPEAKING THROUGH THE HOME*

Attic	Higher mind, consciousness, heart feeling
Second Level	Intuitive nature, heart centeredness, intimacy to Self
Main Level	Relationships, creativity, power, will
Basement	Your foundation, belief systems, thoughts

*If a home only has a main floor, the areas are all on one floor but pertain to each room.

SPEAKING THROUGH HOME-RELATED ISSUES

Cracks – Breaks	Fractured thinking. Misalignment of thoughts and feelings.
Bursts – Blowouts	Intense anger or similar emotion being built up.
Fire – Burnouts	Endings and beginnings. Birthing of a new experience. Phoenix is rising.
Flood – Leaks	Abundance is on its way. The space has been cleansed. Transformation is in process.
Rot – Mold	Belief systems and negative thinking are overtaking your life.
Infestation	Negative thoughts, little things or unsupportive beliefs are gnawing away at you.
Clouding – Fogging	Lack of vision

SPECIFIC ROOMS SPEAKING

Kitchen / Dining	Nourishment, Desire, Fulfillment, Power Center
Bathrooms	Emotional Center, Cleansing, Clearing, Detoxing

Bedroom	Connection to Self. Intimacy to Self.
Living Room / Den	Relationships. Money. Boundaries.
Sun Room	Related to personal power and will. Presence in the world.
Sacred Space	Intuitive Nature. Time for Self.
Garage	Mobility of choices. Unable to move forward or back up.
Plumbing	Emotional blockages.
Roof	Consciousness. Overarching Generational Consciousness and Belief Systems
Driveway	Foundational issues of thought and belief. Wanting to escape.
Pool	Emotional body. Underbelly of emotional nature from generations

Jose and Monica's Story

Jose and Monica, friends of mine, had been wanting to move for several years. They finally decided to put their home on the market. After a few years of challenge and marital difficulty, they decided a fresh start was in order. Both had done a lot of internal work on themselves to grow more conscious and establish a healthier, less codependent relationship.

They had quite a few showings but no real interest. The realtor decided to have an open house, inviting all the other agents in to take a look.

The evening before the event, they both heard a loud pop and all of a sudden water was seeping out of one of the baseboards on the main level of the two-story home. Jose ran upstairs to see where the leak was coming from. Monica went to the basement to see if it was going all the way down.

Jose could find no signs of water leaking or damage. Monica reached the basement to find all the light fixtures flooded and water pouring in. The basement was flooding. Neither could find the source of the water to shut it off and called a plumber to come immediately.

I happened by in the midst of the seeming chaos. I was dropping off some items Monica wanted to borrow for the open house. Monica was distraught. As she was explaining what had happened, the plumber came in and quickly was able to shut off the water. However, the basement was completely flooded. Monica was panicked because there was no way to cancel the event. The realtor suggested they rope off the basement.

As I sat with her, Monica spoke, "This is a sign. This is bad. How could this happen?"

"Why do you think it is bad?" I replied.

"My basement flooded. There is a pipe somewhere in the walls that has burst. How could it be good? It is going to be another expense."

"Monica, let me tell you what I see. YOU both have done an incredible amount of inner work over the last few years. You are ready to move. Your home has illustrated that your foundation is now clean. The flooding happened in the basement. All of this water came from above, meaning you have healed your consciousness and abundance will now flow into your life. It does not have to be bad. In the universe, there is only good if you will see that. However, if you want to see it negatively, you will reverse the abundance that is about to show up."

She looked at me quite perplexed. "Do you really believe that?"

"Trust me. Try to see that this is all good. Be grateful that the Universe has showered abundance on you and see what happens in the midst of that gratitude."

A couple of days later, Monica came by to return the trays she had borrowed. "You are not going to believe it. Well, actually, you will. We had the open house and about twenty realtors showed up. One of them brought a client with her. They put a contract on the house. They actually walked through the basement, with all of the fans blowing and the woman wanted the house anyway. You were right. It was a good sign! Thanks for setting me straight."

16

The Moving Body

Your car is an extension of you. It will give you a tremendous amount of messages. The most important thing to recognize is that it, too, is attempting to lead you back inside yourself. The ultimate goal for everything in your life is for the purposes of mirroring something on the outside that is a reflection of an internal perspective calling out for love.

The vehicles we drive are illustrative of the thoughts and beliefs, feelings and emotions that are on the move in your life. Your vehicle is showing you where you are going or where you need to go. It is not unlike the body in how it correlates to the pieces and parts of us.

Your car is divided into masculine and feminine, past and future. The right side will denote issues stemming from the masculine aspect of your experience. These may be of your own doing or they may be related to the masculine influences in your life or unhealed relations with a male parent or caregiver. The left side reflects the feminine aspect: your ability to receive, the feminine influences in your world, and unhealed issues with a mother or female caregiver.

The front end has to do with where you are headed, your future. The back end of your car reflects your past issues that need to be looked at. Your energy will develop a physical manifestation in your car to help you understand what is in control of your life so that it does not have to affect your physical health. If willing to receive the message, you can avoid a certain degree of health issues.

I know whenever I receive a speeding ticket, I am being told to slow down, both on the highway and in my life. Sometimes we are speeding so quickly through life that the real reason for being here can be forgotten. A speeding ticket is a small pebble in your path telling you to slow down, take the time to reflect, and stop for a moment.

I also have an issue with tires deflating. Typically it is always the right front tire. This has to do with receiving my feminine nature and placing it in the elements in my life to fill myself up. In adding air to the tire, I am always reminded to breathe deeply into myself so that I can tap into the feminine essence that I am. The resource section lists an excellent book that goes into the details of a car. It also identifies how it is completely related to the healing journey of the soul.

I found this to be true on my own, as I pieced together all the parts of me showing up as me. In finding a resource that confirmed my perspective, I realized how much transformation can occur if a person simply pays attention. Your car is important in your soul growth.

Don't take for granted the power of its presence in your life. The color you chose, the name of the car, the issues affecting it, and how you treat it are all messages about yourself. How much attention do you pay to your car? Do you take care of it? Do you service and clean it? Do you drive gently or recklessly? Has it been beat up or cherished?

Whether it is a fender bender, a flat, the engine stops, the air conditioning goes out, or you have an accident, notice what is going on in your life at the time. Be cognizant of your thoughts and feelings. Become aware of how your vehicle is talking to you. Be cognizant of how you run from the past or are speeding into your future. Acknowledge when you are losing air, getting overheated, or running out of gas. Your car is YOU and it is another way the Universe is talking to you about YOU.

Mark's Story

Mark always had to be independent. He had been on his own since the age of sixteen. Somehow things never worked out, but it was not for a lack of trying. He held four jobs, was always working, and had little time for much else. No matter what he did, it was paycheck to paycheck. However, he knew his lucky moment had to be around the corner.

Mark's personality exuded generosity and kindness. He was always jovial and ready to help another but never asked for help. None of his friends knew of his struggle or how alone he felt. He constantly stayed busy to avoid his own discomfort and the truth of his experience.

One day after offering to help a friend move, he was driving back home when he was hit in the rear by another car, completely crumpling his back left side. Mark's car was hit in a way that he spun and went head first into the left side guardrail, also tearing up the front end of the car. The car began smoking immediately and he got out of the car. It had caught on fire. Help soon arrived and the car was taken away; it was completely totaled. He was taken to the hospital after suffering a back injury, broken nose, and burns to the front of his body from the air bag releasing.

Mark had lost his mother as a young child and had never received the nurturing care he wanted or needed. He had grown up trying to earn the love of his father, who was an alcoholic. Needless to say, he never could and ran away at sixteen. The past was being reflected in the left side, the maternal and the need to receive.

The front crash reflected where he was headed. By not stopping to change his inability to receive assistance, his life would begin caving in if he refused to listen. Internally, he held a tremendous amount of rage, signified by the smoking of the car and eventual fire. The burns on his body reflected his self-directed anger as well. He did not want to face himself or his issues. The back injury confirms the lack of support he felt.

This moment was intended to get Mark to stop, even to breakdown . . . and open. The heart must break for true healing to happen. In the midst of all this seemingly extra pressure, Mark had to crumble just like his car. He finally had to ask for help and receive assistance. In the end, the incident with the car would be of service to him. Mark began making changes in his life to be more supported. In doing so, other channels began opening up, bringing him more stability and peace.

This all occurred because Mark took the time to reflect while in the hospital. He stopped long enough to look at his life and himself.

Review of Language Play: Adjectives

Language Play supports opening yourself to integration of your experience. These inquiries assist you in learning your language with the universe. This is not work. It is play, to be engaged in with curiosity and adventure. You will develop the mechanics necessary to more easily have your conversation with the Universe.

Language Play of Adjectives provides the descriptives within the conversational structure that your life is using to speak to you. These let you focus in on the core issues that require your attention and inner work. Nothing is random. Everything in your experience is appearing for your highest good. These things are not only here for you, but as you and the overall experience of you.

The Human Body

- What are the health issues you deal with regularly?
- What health issues surround you and the ones closest to you?
- What do all of these tell you about you?
- Which side of the body do most of your ailments tend to occur on?
- What feeling arises when focusing on the individual ailments?

The Home Body

- Where have your home repairs concentrated?
- Is there a recurring experience in the home?
- How has the home reflected your life experience?

The Moving Body

- What are the issues that have arisen with your car?
- Are they issues relating to the future or the past?
- What feelings are trying to be seen through your car issues?

17

The Punctuation

Have you ever noticed how lessons seem to repeat? Have you had the same experiences show up in your life again and again with different bodies and faces, perhaps with different scenery and places? Have you seen how people who leave relationships tend to find themselves in the same scenario but with a new person? Maybe it has occurred to you that the issue that you had with a parent or caregiver seems to reincarnate through like personalities in the future. How do they keep finding you? Why do they?

If we look at the experiences in our lives in terms of a language, all language has punctuation. There is a timing, frequency, and intensity to everything. The Universe is trying to get your attention and frankly, you can be a little dense sometimes. With that being said, some things have to be said again and again. First they are whispered. Next, you will hear it in a gentle voice. Then, they are spoken firmly. But there will come a moment, if you continue not to listen, when it is said with a strong exclamation.

The Universe is not yelling at you, YOU are strongly nudging you awake. YOU have spent time sending pebbles that would provide a gentle push. YOU have sent rocks that were to put you into action in some way. YOU have sent boulders because you just could not get it. It is up to you to determine the degree of punctuation you require. You have a choice every time to walk on or wake up. Neither choice is wrong or bad, but one may not be as comfortable as the other in terms of its manifestation as experience. Waking up may push you to your limits but it is intended to get you to the place of limitlessness where you can experience your joy.

You are a powerful being that manifests greatly. Human experience had equated growth and evolution with pain and struggle. This does not have to be the case. You have a choice to change that for yourself. It requires you to become aware and awake to your internal landscape. This landscape holds your feelings, beliefs, and intentions, many of which are unknown to you.

If your experience is appearing as exclamation after exclamation, you have to wonder if this has something to do with how you are hearing. If the voices have to speak louder to get your attention, you are not listening. The fact is, strong messages do come as whispers. The real message in an exclamation is that there is a belief in pain, struggle, and a lack of value.

Let the outer landscape provide punctuation that supports a calm conversation. Allow inner reflection to have more of your experiential statements end with a period of space rather than an exclamation. This will occur more gently and easily as you discover that when you are in question, YOU are the answer.

18

Timing

Everything does happen in its own time. It is a combination of your suppressed beliefs and emotions, conscious and unconscious intentions, actions and emotions. These are all timing components. They are part of the human condition. Mind you, the experience is not the condition but the holding of experience in time is the condition. Would these components be necessary if you were fully present and engaged in your spiritual essence?

Flow is a natural experience of the Universe. In that place there is no time; there just is. Timing only happens when we block the natural flow. It occurs in the experiences of control, manipulation, anger, or pain and the subsequent preoccupation of the mind to keep record of it. That is the occupation of the mind. It must have a job, so it records and files. It stops what would be the natural flow until you stop and look back at what was causing the blockage. It is the reason such a thing as his-tory or her-story ever came into being.

Drop It

What is being held in the recesses of your mind? What has been filed and locked away? What has been the undercurrent of your existence? What are the underpinnings that hold you and your life back? It is the mind. It is only doing its job. But you are not the job; you hold the essence of self-love, compassion, and freedom.

Drop from the mind to the eyes and see what happened. Revisit the scenarios that filed away pain, remorse, regret, anger, disillusionment. See what you have not been willing to see. Be with the images that you thought were too much to hold.

Drop from the eyes to the ears and listen to what you have been telling yourself about what you saw. Hear the statements of anger, angst, turmoil, confusion, and friction. Listen to what your inner self has longed to share with you and let that part of you finally be heard with the ears of presence and compassion.

Drop from the ears to the throat and say the words you have longed to express. Give sound to what you saw and heard. State your needs, desires, passions, longings, and withholdings—say your "peace." Speak for and speak forth the person you have been and the person that is birthing.

Drop into the heart and feel what you never let yourself feel before. Open . . . open into your heart space. Feel all the emotions flow forth as a waterfall, let this shower of liquid heal and break away the calcified and hardened places within the heart. Let the waters of healing soften and smooth the ragged edges and sharp points that life experiences have built up. Let the heart bleed forth so the dis-ease may release and new blood pump through.

Move powerfully into the gut. Feel the power that has been sitting there waiting. What stirs within you, ready to be released? What has been held down by the forces of time? What power has lain dormant that urges to reveal itself now? Tap into that presence of YOU and take it down through the feet. Let it pool into the legs and feel your presence. Allow it to seep into the earth, growing roots that extend deeply. You are rooted and strong. Your roots spread deep and wide. You are now grounded.

We are only meant to be in the NOW. There is nothing else. You have created time by placing bookmarks in your great novel of life. You keep going back to that page and rereading it but do not move forward in the story. That bookmark helps you replay the scenario again and again. Soon, you have five, ten, fifteen bookmarks in your story on the same subject. If you keep doing this, your story will never end.

The story needs to end so you can get on with the novel. Timing of your experiences is really the Universe saying, "It's about time you stopped the clock on this." The Universe is providing the alarm in your life to wake you up. Will you wake up early or late? When will you choose to stop the alarm instead of snoozing your way through life? What hour will be the hour you say, "I don't have time for this anymore"?

The moment you choose to stop time and reflect on the places you keep in history, you will free yourself from the time clock you have been punching. Let go of keeping the scorecard. No one wins when there is one, it's just a means to keep the game going. Your grasp of time keeps wounds in place. Let the hands of time go and you will discover YOU are timeless. Then you will be living in the NOW . . . and in the KNOW.

Jackie's Story

Jackie had been at her wits end. Life seemed to be dealing her a bum hand and she had no idea why. She had done everything right. She helped push her husband toward success, sending him to the right school, establishing his business in a certain way, ensuring his success with her guidance. However, twelve years later, he left everything. He left Jackie and the business, stating he wanted no part of her. At that time they had two small children.

As they were growing up, she made sure the children had everything they needed. They were schooled properly. They were guided into the appropriate careers. She even had helped steer them toward good life partners. Both children were successful, but worked all of the time. She had lost connection to them and tried to be very connected to their spouses. Their wives did not like her being involved in their lives. She could not understand because she always tried to push them in directions that were good for them.

Shortly after her husband left the family she was diagnosed with early-stage Parkinson's disease. She felt tremors but was determined to not allow the disease to reach a later stage. Managing to keep it at bay, Jackie went about her life as usual.

Then, a couple of years later, she had a major car accident. The car was totaled. An eighteen-wheeler plowed into her from behind, sending her car spinning and flipping over. She broke both arms, both legs, and several ribs. She was incapacitated for months and had little mobility even after recovery.

She felt alone and afraid. As I sat with her, I could see the landscape. It was so clear, but she had no idea. She had had the string of messages along the way. However in ignoring them, she created circumstances that were literally screaming, "Stop and let go."

It would take several months to help Jackie see the dots that needed to connect, but she eventually realized how this was all created.

Parkinson's is a disease stemming from the emotional cause of feeling the need to control. It was what she had done all of her life. She had controlled her husband's life and business. His leaving was the small pebble that was whispering, "Stop, look at what just happened here. Why did it happen? What was your role in it playing out this way? Why did he leave you and the business?" But she only kept doing what she always did.

Her need to control placed its attention on her children. Once they were out of the house, it focused on their wives. The disconnection to her boys and their families was a larger pebble, a rock. This one was saying, "Stop. Look. Listen. Why are they leaving you as well? What just happened here? Why did it happen? What was your role in it playing out this way?" Jackie kept doing what she always did.

Then a larger rock hit. When the Parkinson's appeared, Jackie was more interested in controlling her health than listening to her body. The mission was about getting rid of the Parkinson's instead of taking care of her Self. Her shaking hands were trying to say, "Let go! Shake loose these things you grip to! Drop everything you have needed to hold!" Instead, Jackie wanted to tell the doctors what needed to be done. She told alternative practitioners how she needed to heal. Parkinson's disease was her new object of control.

The accident was the boulder. It literally ran into her from behind. The past was ramming its way into her to get her to stop. The accident was saying, "Look back! Look behind you. See what happened that is so large. Why have you been spinning, round and round? What is asking you to flip over, completely upside down, in how you see, hear, and behave?"

Furthermore, a huge statement came in the name wrapped on the van: White Flag Pest Control. White Flag is a symbol of surrender. Pest Control speaks for itself. Her body was speaking as well. It had many messages in the breaks. The arms asked her to break through what she held onto. Her legs told her to break her steps and pace. The accident screamed, "Stop now! Sit still! I will not let you grab hold of anything. Give your arms a break! Cast off the things you have been holding onto. Be your own star instead of shining your intense light on everyone else! Trust the pace being asked of you."

Jackie, in her infinite ability to create, had designed her story to completely stop her in her tracks, take away all control, and leave her with herself. However, her healing would require the choice to do so. It would require the courage and discipline to recognize her role in the story. In addition, if she allowed herself to be open to the signs, she would be guided. Healing would and could happen in all realms of her life if she would let herself shift. With a personal shift, all else would shift as well.

19

Thought

The interesting thing about the journey of the Soul and the ability we have to converse with the Universe is that it just happens naturally. Are you able to see it? Will you identify what is revealing or will you send it back down into your depths until another experience bubbles it back up?

I want you to understand how you are conversing with the Universe beyond the affirmations, intentions, and visualizations you activate. This is louder than any words you speak, demands you make, or prayers you breathe out. And these determine what you are creating, how you are creating, and what is really asking for healing.

Whenever an experience occurs that triggers you in some way, there will be a thought, or series of thoughts, that you have at the moment of the experience. This is what you really believe, the space you are really creating from. These are thoughts that normally may be repressed or unconscious. This is the dialogue you are really speaking back to the Universe. You are asking the Universe to continue proving this to you through its language and creations.

It is your first response that is your truth in that moment. It is a gauge you can always trust if you want deeper knowledge of your Self. If you want to change your current experience, you must know what is on the tip of your tongue in those moments that trigger. You are creating from the moment of now, even if that now moment is attached to a then experience. If you choose to look at it, reflect on it, heal it, and integrate the healing on all levels, you move the then moment to a Zen moment. In other words, constantly doing this sort of work will keep you in the "now and Zen."

20

Feeling

Your greatest guidance system is your feeling nature. You are a composite of vibrations that range in scale from density to Light. That is what makes up the whole of YOU, the whole of the YOUniverse. There is no right or wrong feeling, no good or bad experience, not even a positive or negative expression. There is only a range of frequencies to be felt, experienced, and expressed. Your mind has computed it incorrectly. You have believed you are experiencing circumstances that create feelings. You have believed when you are in the midst of sadness or anger or happiness or joy that others have affected you. You believe you are experiencing pain or bliss because of them. Is that true? Do the things on the outside hold that much power?

Perhaps it is best to view it in a different light. Could feeling have existed first? Has it been seeking to express itself? Has its creative impulse desired to manifest into experiencing? What if the emotions are actually experience birthing experiencing as you? What if sadness is moving through your body and your life to experience unfolding, action, reaction, response, and reintegration? This experiencing could manifest in many ways: suppressed emotion, tears, words, action, service toward humanity. This would be the experiencing continuing as experience. It is all creation. Suppressed emotion creates as dis-ease, experiencing manipulation of the physical form, expanding into new experience. Expressed emotion creates healing, allowing expansion of the heart and creative capacity for expansion of experience. Action ripples out into the world as experiencing for many, ever expanding the intensity of emotion multiplying into many forms: greater upset, forgiveness, healing, or love. In all of these cases, you are the experiencing. Your interpretation of having any emotion or being affected by emotion is the experience of experiencing.

Do you create feeling or does it already exist to channel itself through you? Did you come before Love or did Love create you for the purpose of experiencing itself? In the midst of joy, happiness, or love, do you think you are those things? Or is love experiencing how you respond to it moving through you? Are you responding to your experience of it? Is joy experiencing you as smiles, laughter, and generosity? Does happiness fill you? And then do you giggle, laugh, float, dance, sing, and create? Happiness is experiencing. You are experience. The giggle, laugh, float, dance, song, and creation are experiencing. Your actions from there are experience. The new creation that manifests is experience. It will find a way to again become experiencing. Your body, personality, identity, and human nature are always the experiencing. But you are so much more than that. You are feeling that is expansive, never-ending, infinite.

The deeper you allow the experiencing of feeling through you, the greater access you have to the field of feeling that exists. All is simply energy. Your degree of expansion is relative to your level of having feeling come through you. When you expand as feeling capacity, you possess the power to feel into those around you, those at a distance, and even those across the world. You have the ability to feel the feeling essence of trees and animals. It is energy, an essence, a field of oneness within and surrounding all things. Feeling is what is attracting. It is your oneness connection within the field. This is the real meaning of the law of attraction. You are attracting YOU to you, feeling to feeling, like frequency to like frequency.

The law of attraction does not bring you signs, symbols, language, lessons, and experiences based on what you are thinking. This language manifests based on what you are feeling. The mind is merely the computer. It is for storing, analyzing, and computing. The heart is for feeling, attracting, and creation.

The Universe is always asking you, "What do you feel like today?" It then sends that to you. The conversation always begins with your experiencing and when you respond, the Universe experiences itself in, as, and through you again and again and again. Stop trying to run from your emotions. Do not attempt to avoid certain experiences. It is all to be had. And once it has been, it does not need repeating. There may be a similar experiencing but it will always come with a unique difference. There must always be creative capacity and evolution. Growth and change are the natural path of "feeling" through the Universe.

Review of Language Play: Punctuation

Language Play supports opening yourself to integration of your experience. These inquiries assist you in learning your language with the universe. This is not work. It is play, to be engaged in with curiosity and adventure. You will develop the mechanics necessary to more easily have your conversation with the Universe.

Language Play of Punctuation provides the emphasis of the conversation. These inquiries give the degree of attention being asked for within the conversational structure that your life is using to speak to you. Nothing is random. Everything in your experience is appearing for your highest good. These things are not only here for you, but as you and the overall experience of you.

Pebbles, Rocks, & Boulders

- Identify the pebbles, rocks, and boulders that have appeared in your life as messages.
- What patterns occur before these various stages?
- What are the messages that appear in the midst of these patterns?
- What are the cycles and rhythms of your life? Take the time to write your life story.

Timing

- Is there a timing sequence to what you create in your life?
- Where have you placed your bookmarks in life?
- What are the experiences that have been filed in the mind?

- What takes you to the past, the should-haves, the could-haves?
- Use the 'Drop It' exercise for every bookmark that appears.

Thought

- When triggered, note statements that immediately enter the mind.
- Write the judgments about the experience, the person involved, or the self.
- Use the 'Drop It' exercise for each of these thoughts. Feel into your Self.
- Choose a new belief to breathe in and integrate.
- Take the new beliefs into the heart and feel into them.

Feeling

- What are the feelings that regularly rise up from within?
- Which of these feelings do you continually push down, ignore or dislike?
- Are your experiences asking you to face and embrace these particular feelings?
- What seems to be missing from your experience that causes those feelings to appear?
- Is the conversation the universe is having with you asking you to fill your own needs regarding these feelings? If so what would that look like as the language of experience.
- Can you allow yourself to let all feelings rise up and just be with them? When you do this, what happens?

PART THREE

The Integration of
Universal Language

21

The Language

There is so much in the world that is neither seen, heard, nor given presence to. An individual can only know life based on the filters and perceptions they see through. These filters stem from our childhood and generational influences. We are a composite of past experience and the interpretations that built on top of them. But we are given the gift of choice. Will you choose more of yourself?

The richness of YOU cannot fully exist until you touch it. The blessings and various expressions of YOU that exist in your world cannot speak to you until you give them presence in your life. The Universe desires for you to experience the full expanse of Love, but it will be unavailable until you become available to your Self. YOU are Love. Immerse yourself in love and in the language of love. This is the language the Universe creates and speaks from. Love is everything that exists.

Open the heart a little more each day. See the Self more liberally in every way. Touch your passion, honor your loving essence, dive into your full nature and you will discover a different language than the one you have always heard. You will discover a whole new world. Life will begin changing from black and white to full-blown color. Limiting perceptions limits how we see. The vocabulary of fear keeps individuals locked in a language that is conditional. This will result in a love that is also conditional. That is why it is known as the human condition, one of separation and misunderstanding.

Everything in your creation has been created in and with Love. Each time you choose to expand yourself and be "In Love" with any part of creation, the illusion of conditions and separations is brought back home fully into unconditional love. As you as a being of Love learn to be in love with the self, this self-love shall continue to create in its own image creating a world populated by reflections of the self.

Traditional perception-based language does not always serve greater truth. It holds distortion, interpretation, inflection, and its own manner of interpretation by the listener. The energy taken to understand words and seek meaning behind the intentions, motives, and manipulations is part of the freezing process. It can be the block that creates stuckness, the in-dwelling of illusion. It is where we stay stuck in the head rather than dropping a few inches into the heart, and a few more into the core. It is why there is a need to delve more deeply.

The language of symbolism resonates with the truth of the soul. Of course, it can be colored when we attempt to use the mind to figure it out, but when moving with the wonder and the feeling heart of an inno-cent child, it can only reveal itself as truth guiding us to individualized Truth.

The language of the Universe will appear in whatever manner you need to see it. It will incorporate any object, initiate any experience, and utilize timing for the greatest chance of your good. It is always present to and for you. There is a language specifically for you. It may look and seem like the same for others, however it will be designed to fit your unique perceptions, feelings, and desires. In various moments of chal-lenge or ease, any instance that the journey need reach in a stronger way toward the soul's intent, there will be full sentences and paragraphs guiding the way. If you are willing to connect the synchronicities, the Universe's version of words, the conversation will be ongoing.

Oneness, also known as this ongoing conversation, endures consist-ently and wholly even within the world of duality. You are just taught to see it all as separate until you begin to wake up and really see its fullness. Once you discover this magical synchronicity, your soul will expand with excitement, even in moments you think you need to get your vision and hearing checked. As you achieve a greater knowing and understanding of your true soul nature and trust the language being spoken to you, the walk between the worlds will reveal, with equal awareness, upon both.

Before you were born, you had an intention. You said, "Do not let me get lost. Place the signs along the way that lead me back home to center. Give me the opportunity to fragment as much as needed to become my own language. Create a me that I can piece together. In that dialogue, I shall discover my connection and oneness, fully remembering myself. I shall pick up the signs, symbols, and synchronicities along the way as pieces and parts of myself wanting to come home. I shall put the puzzle of me back together."

In doing so, YOU become the tree that falls, the butterfly that crosses your path, the dog that barks. YOU are the knee pain, the cough, and the blurred vision. YOU are the leaky faucet, the rotting floorboard, and the clogged plumbing. YOU are the flat tire, the fender bender, and the empty gas tank. YOU are the angry store clerk, the admired celebrity, and the innocent baby in your arms. YOU hold the ability to change with the seasons and the seasons changing. Each of these is a word, symbolic of a noun, verb, or adjective that has come together to form sentences and paragraphs of YOU communicating with yourself. These mirrors, these aspects of Self, are revealing YOU to you. They are love manifest and can only be go(o)d.

Ask yourself: "What do these things symbolize to me? How do they make me feel? If there is only go(o)d, what is the go(o)d this is speaking into me? Where am I in this and where is it in me?" Love can be anywhere it likes. It creates anything and everything it desires. YOU are Love. Love embellishes what you do not understand and YOU use a massive variety of symbols to play this out.

The fact is, you are creation creating itself. You were created in the image of the Creator. You have the Creator's very makeup, DNA, essence—YOU are that. In that essence of creative ability, would Father-Mother Creation not bestow upon its child its own inherent qualities and gifts? Would its child not be a reflection and carry on the legacy from which it came? This is your inheritance. Creation allows you to inherently touch and express this Divine lineage. "Honor thy Mother and thy Father." What better way than to honor, experience, and express each and every gift that was bestowed upon you?

22

The Moment

Life may seem as if it would have you wander about without any clue or sense as to where you are going. In fact, you are being guided always in all ways and if you disconnect your brain, you will be able to discern this. The areas of darkness you traverse appear unmarked but they are filled with the appropriate signs to direct you out of the dark night. As you call in your truth in your own way—begging, praying, stomping, screaming, or breaking down—the surrendered self will begin looking and opening to what is there. It is innate within your cellular structure to recognize, remember, and reconnect. The heart will open and a new day will dawn. You will begin to see, precisely placed, the signs, instructions, directions, indications, and promptings that guide you to your next best, most appropriate step.

These things, as you have seen, can come in a variety of expressions from a protruding boulder that lands in your path to a giant billboard staring you in the face. You will receive the answer you seek in each moment if you open to the innocent surprise, synchronicity, and magic available to you. The message will appear in whatever manner you need to see it. You need only be aware.

Whenever you allow yourself the stance of innocence and childlike wonder, even in the midst of your anxiety, stress, and skepticism, you will cross from the edge of your current illusion to something very real. In the next moment of your experience, the answer will blaze brightly in front of you. Let yourself catch it. Do not miss life happening for YOU. Everything has been placed, waiting to be received. The language will light up, come forward, or seem bigger than everything else around it.

Let yourself rest from the speed of life. As you move to a slower pace, breathing in what is around you, your eyes shall open to things you have not let yourself see. Rest without the need to know and breathe in what is revealed. Imagine you are new, born again innocent, waiting to inhale the wonder of anything and everything that comes upon your path. Notice what you are introduced to in each moment and see how it plays out in melody, a tune, your song of the soul. Your song is playing without you ever having been introduced to it before. It is natural and organic, as is your life and your guidance. Touch the perfect beauty and magic of this new world. From a neutral space, without the judgments of good or bad, allow yourself to see the opportunities of love's synchronistic expression beckoning you to have a dialogue.

In each moment that you choose Love, engage in the dialogue, and open your heart, your experience transforms. You become part of the great conversation that is. Instead of listening to it or looking for it, you become part of it.

23

Putting It Together

Before you become frantic or establish a neurotic sense of trying to find things to look at or search every book and the internet for the meanings of things coming into your awareness, relax. This is a process of gentleness, ease, and play. It can only be had in fun. A sense of humor is required. Approach every condition and circumstance with less seriousness. You are not to push your way into a conversation. It need not be demanded or even coerced, it will just happen. This is an awakening process. Awaken. Awaken to your own sense of presence.

How much more present can you be today than yesterday. Initially, be present to you. Move gently. Move slowly. Feel each movement, each breath, and each touch. Discover how your lips move when they speak, how your legs step when you walk, how your arms extend when you reach. How you do one thing is how you do everything. The way you speak, act, and interact is the way the Universe will converse with you. Why? Because it knows you and knows your journey is to know your Self. It will only reflect YOU back to you.

As you become more present to your own being in the world—your thoughts and feelings and actions—awakening will begin. Your eye will catch objects, symbols, signs, coincidence, and synchronicity because you are beginning to see your Self. You may not know it as YOU yet, but you will come to know precisely that.

Putting the language together will create the ongoing dialogue. As you connect the dots, you will feel connected to more and more. In time you will experience the conversation as continuous. You will be able to discern what happenings are related to which events in your life. You will also discover that your experiences in different areas of your life are connected. As you begin to see a shift in one area of your experience, do not be surprised if the other areas of life also improve.

Initially, of course, you may get caught up in looking up every little thing that appears. It is alright to get a linear understanding of what is being said. Everything is a process and you are the journey. Integrative heart-gut comprehension is what will change your world. But definitely take advantage of the resources that help bring meaning to things. My intention is for you to develop your connection in a greater way. I desire for you to go deeply in its understanding and personal knowing, beyond mere intellectual comprehension. Feel it.

There are three methods of discerning the parts of language. You may engage in one or all of them. Choose to spend a certain period of time for each, as if learning a new language curriculum. The method chosen is not important but your presence to "what is" matters. Do not get too caught up in the how. My desire is for you to learn to trust your intuition and take the first thought that comes to mind every single time. That is always your soul speaking to you.

Universal communication in your external world is not meant to keep you focused on the outside. Its sole intention is for you to always carry that language back to the inside of who you are. It is the mirror. If you desire to touch that thing on the outside or know it in a deeper way, you would not reach for the mirror would you? No, you would reach for the self and adjust or touch that area.

The outside world is composed of your accessories. They are here to dress your experience. They create the sparkle and the sizzle, the utility and the warmth. Your outer garments will continuously change. According to your need, they are all "on" you. Your outer wares are what you are wearing. You need only be willing to discover, "where" are they in me?

Method 1:

Keep a journal of what your eye randomly catches and holds. Also list the things that give you "aha" moments, a word or inspiration that makes you feel something. Notice what crosses your path, those moments that make you say, "Look at that . . ." Get used to what your common words are by seeing what keeps repeating or giving you a repeat feeling or thought.

Method 2:

Whenever you have an issue or just want assistance along the path, ask one question out loud with intention. Then request that the specific guidance appear that can guide you in discerning the answer. Take note of the things that happen during the day and how they connect to your question. Be cognizant of the songs, books, or words of others. What does your eye catch? What experience happens in your own life on that day? It will be the greatest clue as to the mindset, feeling set, and action set to follow.

Method 3:

Notice what comes your way. Stop for a moment and close your eyes. Notice how you feel in this moment. Connect to where it is in your body. Breathe that space and hear its first comment. Breathe deeply upon that. Repeat that statement out loud. Does it resonate? You will feel confirmation in your body if it does.

Go deeper in your senses and gauge if any other sense is activated. If so, sit with it and allow it to guide you into contemplation. Feel within the heart where it desires to lead you.

Now, ask yourself what this symbol, person, or experience is trying to show you about YOU. What high quality is being signified that you can embody and incorporate right now into your life? Take the steps to integrate that action, characteristic, or mannerism into your life through small steps in word, thought, feeling into it, and action. Be as present to life in this manner as you can. Don't rush it. Do not judge yourself or think it needs to be at a certain speed. Just allow "you" as the journey being experienced, and breathe "you" in slowly and deeply. Any other way, especially through force, creates resistance.

24

The Response

You may be wondering, "What do I do with all of this information? How do I figure out what symbol goes where and how to read it? Will I not just be more confused and neurotic than ever?"

Do not look at this as something else to do. This is to help you understand that there is more of you to be aware of. This is not a report that you are researching. If you want to know what specific things mean, there are plenty of books listed in the resources section that will help you do that. This is about you connecting to your intuition. There will come a point where you realize you do not need to look anything up; you will begin gaining an understanding of what things mean.

The guides are a good reference of standard meanings that fit all people. However, you will discover that the Universe has a unique dialect just for you.

It will take the standard meanings deeper or put a twist on them that is only intended for your understanding. This will also let you look at the lives of others and interpret what is happening. Just have fun with it. Interact with the world in a new way.

This is an opportunity for you to be present to what is around you touching you all the time: energy, air, smells, sights, sounds, and tastes. You will first be getting acquainted with this. Then, you will see parts that you desire to know a little more and they will begin to show up a more frequently. There will be parts you are able to have long drawn out conversations with while other pieces will be strangers for a while. There will be some that seem like loud blaring voices on a megaphone. Soft whispers will grace you as well.

How many pieces of YOU are you willing to know and how intimately will you know your Self? Will you keep these voices at a distance? Will they be mere acquaintances or will they become close friends or soul family? Will you release the voices of the mind? Could everything be a representation of YOU? Could this really be one grand celebration of YOU?

Know your place. Know your place as a human being, as a spiritual being, and as a catalyst for change. Know your place as Love in essence and action. Know your Self as the whole, appearing separate but, completely as ONE.

Can you step beyond yourself and let someone or something go for the greater knowing of Truth . . . your truth? Even if it is something you truly Love? Sometimes it is easy to fall in love with the version of the self you have come to know. You may have gotten so comfortable in your life of challenge, dysfunction, conflict, or chaos that you do not notice the discomfort. Can you release all that you know and step into the unknown? Are you ready to become known?

Love is wise enough to see the greater picture and hold the journey in compassion while acknowledging that time, space, and story are all illusions. You will discover the ideal placement is created for all. Let Love do its thing!

There is truth, there is greater truth, and finally there is TRUTH, DIVINE INFINITE TRUTH. Do not get caught up in your version of the illusion. Do not take things as truth because someone told you it was or it has been that way for ages. Remember, whenever you feel the need to prove your point, state your case, or find evidence in support of your cause, you are trying to convince yourself. In those moments is an opportunity to go from what you perceive as truth to a deeper knowing of truth, to the ultimate TRUTH, beyond what most human minds have been privy to before now.

Truth simply states itself and is confident in that place. TRUTH connects and beholds all things. It does not judge, divide, fight, or inspire fear. Truth is all encompassing. Go deeper on the inside and you will be able to see with broader vision on the outside. Connect in a greater way to what is unknown on the inner landscape and you will experience greater connection in a greater way to the beauty of the outer landscape. You will discover that something is radiating from within and being matched on the outside, because it is all YOU know.

Who makes you feel magnificent? Who makes you feel beautiful? What people bring out your power? Who inspires you? Who lifts you up to be your highest expression? Who believes in you even when you cannot? Who holds you in your lowest moments and your highest success? Who are your cheerleaders? Who loves you unconditionally? What things inspire you?

These are the ones you must stay around; this is your soul-family. They can be animate or inanimate. They can be still or breathing. Choose those that choose YOU, all of you, without the need to change, manipulate, criticize, influence, or judge. Choose those who know and express who they are, so you may know who you are. Choose that which resonates and creates resonance.

Review of Language Play: Integration

Language Play creates an opening within to integrate your experience fully. Each section engages you in inquiry that ultimately supports learning the language of the universe. This is not work. It is play, intended to be engaged in with curiosity and adventure. You will develop the mechanics necessary to more easily have your conversation with the Universe.

Language Play Integration takes all of the previous components of language and what is considered the human experience and asks that it be engaged with on a moment to moment basis, taking into account all of the fields of thought, emotion, action, time and space to be linked together to form the dialogue of creation that is you.

The Language

- How have you begun to notice your language appearing?
- How does it make you feel when it does?
- Are you conscious about going inside each time something shows up or are you living on the outside waiting for the messages?
- To go beyond who you are in the outside world, you must go into the beyond in your inner world.

The Moment

- Are you choosing to wake up now?
- Are you willing to have assistance?
- Are you ready to step out of victimhood, settling, and apathy?
- Engage with the experiences and feelings arising moment by moment.
- Love into all feelings. Hold especially close the ones you want to resist.

Putting it Together

- What matters to you?
- What is your heart asking for that you continually ignore?
- Are the messages showing up every time you contemplate these dreams?
- How much humor do you bring to your experience?
- Do you apply humor to the obstacles as well?

The Response

- Who are the individuals that you admire?
- Who reflects the qualities that you most desire?
- Imagine these individuals at separate times. Tap into what you feel about them. Go inside and find that feeling within yourself. Expand into that.
- Apply these attributes, feelings, and qualities to the expression of your dreams.

PART FOUR

The Soul of Universal Language

25

The Story

The story is what entrances you. It is intriguing and mesmerizing. In choosing a human incarnation, Creation desired that you be a magnificent storyteller. Somewhere along the way, you forgot you were the storyteller and became the story. You got knee-deep in your own script and you have been bogged down ever since, all the while carrying a great scar upon your back, proclaiming victimhood, yet wearing costumes to hide it. This badge of honor allowed you to blame, complain, and criticize. It has been a subtle way to engage in pessimism on the inside while portraying optimism on the outside. It was a way you could remain feeble, small, and lost. It is the illusion. But it is the lie of all lies. Your life is proof of the living lie. Just look at your world—look at the world. Your consciousness is a contributing to the creation. This is not said to cause you guilt, shame, or to blame you, but to wake you up to something no one may have said to you. I love you enough to share with you the shocking truth about myself, about you, about the human condition. You may deny it, but what if it is true? If it's true, you have found the key to being set free.

What happens when one lie is told? Ten more have to be created to keep the first one going. Victimhood provides the landscape to plant a multitude of additional stories. There are so many they begin growing on top of one another like weeds. Pretty soon there are layers upon layers of dense entangled emotions and a massive configuration of lies leading to more stories.

Emotion in itself is good, but when we keep emotion attached to a story, it becomes overgrown and unmanageable. No matter how we cut it back, the roots of what began continue sprouting new weeds within the garden until any flower is choked out. Only when we pull the weeds fully from the landscape does the garden grow. But there comes a point where you grow tired of tending to the garden. You no longer let yourself see the weeds. At this point they become the dis-ease of the human condition, the human condition of victim consciousness. The ground becomes hardened and dry with assumed belief systems, inherited traditions, history, and legacies. These sit at the bottom of the brush affecting the growth of anything beyond.

Victimhood became embedded in your cellular structure long ago. It was the fall from grace, the sin or self-inflicted nonsense, the one that has been calling out as longing for all time. This longing is the greatest mask of victimhood because it is the belief that something is missing and separate.

The victim is the producer of individual "soul reality television" as you play out your own drama, behaving in the very ways you judge others for, enacting the very dysfunction you criticize, becoming the exact people you have pointed a finger at in blame or judgment. Beneath it all is the foundation of pessimism, a tendency to see, anticipate, and emphasize only bad and undesirable outcomes, results, and problems, albeit, for most, an unconscious, hardly noticeable tendency. But it is the doctrine that this world is the worst of all possible worlds, that evil exists, and that pain is required.

If you question or balk at these thoughts, listen to your words during the course of a day. Your words do not lie. See how often you use the words "need," "can't," "should," or "don't have." How often do the thoughts creep in that life is hard, painful, unfair, or against you? How many times do you fear the walls caving in, the other shoe dropping, the people around you, your health failing, or your life changing? How often are you frightened of "your government"? "Your" government?

The outer world is a reflection. How are you governing your life? What is governing your life? Who is really governing your experience? Is it and has it been fear, victimhood, regret, blame, shame, and beliefs that do not serve? What beliefs have you made laws in your own world? What agency and outdated mandates are you allowing a deep-seated false part of you to employ? This story you live by will not let you fully see the truth as long as you deny that something could exist. In order to develop full oneness and connection to all that you are, you must embrace full connection to all that you have denied as yours, including your shadow.

How is it possible to know if this shadow really exists? How do you know if this shadow is convincing you of being the story? The story is the proof of its control and voice. We all begin seeking things to fill us, to have the feeling of being full. We all seek out other people to love us, take care of us, and make us complete, so as not to feel separate. This longing leads us down many paths, seeking many techniques, and following many teachers. We all engage in dogma, fight for what we believe is "the way," and justify pain as a means for growth and evolution. It is not.

Your pain is our own self-created nonsense. It is playing with the victim personality that you have now made your lover. As it pushes and pulls you back and forth between have and have not, you falsely find thrill in the endless roller coaster ride of emotion. You have long been in a codependent relationship with the Self, addicted to your own need for drama and pain as the drug of choice. Why? You do it because you are lost in your own story and have forgotten that YOU are the way out. It is not outside of you, in a guru's special anointing, a trip to a foreign land, a new relationship, acts of service for self-worth, or the accumulation of wealth. It rests deeply in your own structure waiting to be unlocked . . . unleashed.

The Self whispers, "Instead of following many paths, be the path. Instead of searching many truths, see the truth. Instead of listening to many voices, recognize there is one voice. Instead of believing that you are separate and alone, can't you see you are "all-One"? You are not incomplete; acknowledge that you are in completeness. Instead of subscribing to beliefs and taking them as the truth, begin questioning everything, especially that which you dare not. Within the word "believe" are the words "lie" and "live." Be'lie've you can either "be the lie" or "be (a)live." When looking at the word "belief" understand it is asking you to be-lief, to be dear, beloved, and treasured. You have a choice to be the "lie" or the "lief."

When you take on belief systems that are not your truth, you program another opportunity for victimhood to weave new stories and perpetuate the pain of life. Until you have the inner knowing of truth that is not attached to love, approval, or acceptance of anyone else, do not take on beliefs. Know that you are everything else. Know that your being is love, approval, and acceptance. From that place, see the magical synchronous world you have created as depictions of you. Step out of being the story; once again be witness to it. Accept your inheritance and innate connection as reality. From the place of witness, admire this creation in all its magnificence. Acknowledge every detail that has been put in place. Accept your divinity as right in the story of creation. When you lift your own veils of disillusionment, fear, and falsehood, you "will" what is real into your world. Dissolve the stories and just be present, be the present and know you are the present that has been given to this experience. It is time now to get to the root of who you really are.

Whether stuck in your muck and liking it or rewriting your story and becoming the hero, there is magic in your midst. The truth is that there is no separation. For most, this remains an intellectual concept. You have to drop it into the gut and then allow synchronicity and universal language to begin flirting. Rise in love to the place in the high heart that feels a sense of Oneness with all things. Let yourself consider that Creator could have created any possibility and YOU are that. Take advantage of the mystical beautiful magic. Fall into the resonant melody of life being your love song, love story, and a romance of the soul.

The longing is for you to realize you "be longing" for yourself. The one and only that you have been seeking belonging to, is you. All of your longings, despite what they are, really signifiy your own desire to belong and be cherished by you. Don't be longing, belong. You seek to fill your own void with what is already there but you fear, when looking inside, that there is only a black hole, an endless nothingness. The victim mind would say, "I am nothing, there is nothing, therefore I need something. I am empty, I must fill myself up. I am dark, so I need to seek the Light."

The truth of the Self, being hidden by the longing shadow of the victim, knows and patiently waits for you to see what is real. It waits patiently for you to break through your own self-created veils. The Self knows, "I am everything, the vastness of space. I am complete in my ability to create everything I desire. I am the Light with the ability to cast shadow when I consciously choose; and that too is go(o)d. I am form and that which is formless. I am the All, the Is, the Will."

As the victim plays the role of hidden mistress, the Self is the Beloved. We each are the Lover, seeking the Beloved but tantalized by the thrill of the seductive mistress. The romance of the soul is to unite the Lover and Beloved. In that sacred marriage, the One true Self can be found, the ONE that is all that is. We are the ONEs, we are ONE, we are THE ONE.

Some brilliant part of you knew this was the courtship and romance of all time.

Gifts and blessings of the Self are depicted everywhere and in everything. Rising up as messages, symbols, signs, and synchronicity, they proclaim, "Look at yourself. See your Light. Discover your shadow. Know your magnificence. Connect to all that is your being, your reflection, your reincarnation, your representation."

Because you do not seek within, the Self took its most valuable innate Divine trait—that of creation—to assist in the re-membering of It-Self. In the midst of this vast complexity of false victimhood, the Self placed creative clues as to the truth. What is revealed through these magnificent creations that tell you about you is merely the tip of the iceberg. There is a vastness beneath your surface that spans great depths. It begs of your exploration, and your immersion.

The Rainbow Bridge

You are drawn to discover what's waiting out there without yet knowing if you have the courage to face it. You are looking for answers that will satisfy a hunger you have felt for a very long time. Although you may perceive these steps as walking through life and living, they have much more to do with having the courage to die and the courage to die continually. You must die to who you are to give birth to who you can become. The journey we each take is the walk upon a fine line of yes or no, have or have not, to be or not to be, living or dying, death, birth and rebirth.

As I look upon my life, I see there has always been a constant longing. Initially, it began as a longing for acknowledgment, then things, objects of beauty that would allow me to feel my senses. Then it changed to a longing to share and connect with another, but even this never filled it. It evolved into a longing to create and I got busy doing just that. However, I quickly—or not so quickly, depending on how you judge time—realized what I wanted still eluded me.

It had no name, shape, or form. I knew it was out there but did not know what it was. It beckoned me, called to me, seduced me. Yet I clung to my line, the place between living and dying, the place of neutrality, nothingness, a more subtle sense of numbness. I was being drawn to discover it, to meet it, to become intimate with me in the process of finding it. I wanted answers. I wanted to touch my true power, taste who I really was, and know my own truth. I knew it was bigger than I was and would ask of me more than I thought possible to give. Would I be willing to say YES to it, and perhaps NO to everything I had come to know: myself, my life, family, friends, and identity? Could I die to who I was to see who I could become? Could I have the courage . . . to die?

Most would think I was crazy for even considering leaving my life. They would question my sanity for taking the risk and letting go; no one would understand. But they did not need to, it did not concern them. It did not concern anyone else but me. I had died so many times in my forty-four years—more frequently in the last eleven. Could I die yet again, in the greatest possible way this time? Would I be asked to let go of everything? My marriage, identity, children, career, personality, and limitations? My beliefs about who I am and what I could have? Even more so, could I release my preconceived notion of who I was becoming?

I knew if I did not, I would die inside. If I said YES, I would die on the outside. What was the greater of the two sacrifices? Or were they sacrifices at all? If I really looked, was it purely a belief in sacrifice? Dying on the inside would be a sacrifice. Dying on the outside would only be birth; it could only provide something new. At the very least, it would give me an experience of courage and self-love like never before. In the laws of the Universe, such an action can only create equal opposite results and mirrors. All that could result was a reflection of equivalent love. Love would always result in a deeper experience of myself, either my Light or my Shadow. I chose to step into courage, the walk of courage that leads to death. I'll see you on the other side. I will hold the space and wait for you.

YOUR life and life choices do not concern anyone else but YOU. Do not let yourself die on the inside. Instead die to the outside and see what can be birthed anew, more powerful, more courageous, more beautiful and magnificent than you could possible know. You know if it is time, it will have been nagging at you for a while. What will you choose? Can you listen to the voice within asking you for something more, longing for something unknown, asking you to die? Will you listen to the language on the outside, constantly guiding your steps? Follow the rainbow bridge. YOU are the pot of gold at the end. Climb the internal ladder of Light, touch each prism of the rainbow as you step from rung to rung into the highest reaches of your heart, mind, body, and soul. Are you willing to see what happens if you seek to find what rests at the end of the rainbow bridge? You may discover that the vastness of the Universe you thought to exist on the outside cannot compare to the infinite vastness, wealth, beauty, and power that exists inside of you. Leave never-never land for the great escape into ever-ever land where there are only rainbows and light, beautiful music and stars, a grand stage with the ability to have and to hold you in timelessness and as space.

You cannot settle. You cannot settle in life, you cannot settle in love, and you cannot settle in any area of your experience. If you do, you create the block to all that you desire. Ultimately, you block knowing who you really are. You know if you have settled. You may not admit it to yourself for a long time, if ever, but it will give you a feeling, a feeling that everything is okay but something is not quite right. It is a feeling that tries to convince you that where you are is good enough. It will prod you with every reason why it makes no sense to change your current circumstances. But still something will haunt you.

You will look at your life, perhaps others will look at your life, and tell you that you have it good, you should appreciate it, that you should count your blessings and just be content with what you have. But deep down something inside you churns. It has always rumbled and gnawed at your core. It is a knowing that there is something else. It is beyond space and time and it whispers to you beneath the surface. It gives you no promises but provides access to all that is possible. What it speaks of scares you to death because it speaks of your power, your greatness, real love, infinite creativity, and unlimited experiences.

But who are YOU to have all that? How can you know it will come? Can you possibly risk what little—or what all—you have for something that most would view as pipe dreams or impracticalities? If you do not, will you forever wonder "What if?"

You are likely spending your life trying to avoid pain. Don't you know that it is part of why you came? Pain does not exist to be a villain against you. In fact, it is not even here to hurt you; it is here to heal you. Embrace it. Let it be your guide, your teacher, and your heart surgeon. Do not be afraid of pain, it is the key to the locked mysteries of your Self. It is truth's loving voice asking you to wake up and pay attention. It desires you to look within and go deep in a desire to have you grow up your ladder of Light.

It has not come to you from something outside. It has finally had an opportunity to reveal itself because it has been buried deeply within you. It desires to be free, as you do. Don't you see? You have kept the Self prisoner. You have held it down. You have bound it for too long. Your pain only desires to be released and fly out of you so the Self can reveal. If you will just let it go, you will both be Light enough to fly.

Hold pain within your awareness. See it in the molecules of your cells. It is part of you; pieces and parts of you. You say, "I do not want to see it. If I focus on it, I magnify and support it." Please know that the energy you use to deny it is far stronger than the energy required to see it. Your denial of it is what keeps it in place and growing ever stronger in its ability to control your life.

Gently caress every place of discomfort regardless of if it's mental, emotional, physical, or spiritual. Call it out of the shadows. Focus your Light upon it so that it may find its way up and out. Reach for it and softly speak to it. "Why are you hiding here? Is there something you are keeping from me? Do you hold a message I need to hear?" Then lift it into your arms and offer your love. It is an innocent piece of you that has carried such a burden. Does that part of you not deserve love? Has it not been Divine in fulfilling its contract and mission for you, for your own journey of personal growth and healing? Is it not your angel of sacrifice? Did you not request at some place and time for your soul to evolve? Was this not the one piece of you that loved you so deeply, so tenderly, that it would feel intensity in this way for you?

When you chose your healing journey, you brought your own laboratory with you along with lab assistance. Spend each moment looking for truths hidden and buried in the dark. They will appear in many forms: a baby's giggle stuffed beneath an anguished cry, the wind blowing on your skin beneath a raging storm, a butterfly emerging from a cocoon after being stuck and tightly bound. The Universe demands a leap of faith to bear witness to your magnificence. That magnificence is buried under the muck that is weighing down on it. You are urged to recognize cycles and rhythms as you masterfully create them in plain sight. To reach the heights of what you can be, you must dive into the depths of who you are. To be found, be willing to get lost. Let go and let yourself live!

The moment is NOW. Not tomorrow, not next week, or next year—RIGHT NOW! This very moment can alter your destiny but it will require your courage. You will have to be stronger than you have ever been. No one will likely understand your choices; it is not for them to do so. You may not have had any support but you are here to learn that you are all the support you need. No one will cheer you on because they cannot behold the vision you have or they would have achieved their own destiny.

It will require you to let go. You may have to let go of things you have, people you love, habits and beliefs you have collected. It will test your faith, asking you to leap and leap and leap! And you will be asked to trust. The easiest way to know your truth is to live in the moment, taking one step at a time. Block the noise from other people and stay focused on what you know to be true about yourself. What you do not know make up until it can be embodied as your experience.

And finally, know that I am on your side. I walk hand in hand with you. I believe in you. I believe in your dreams. I believe in the amazing novel your soul has written for you to experience. I cannot wait to see your light continually brighten because, my dear, YOU already shine! I stand in applause for who you have been, who you are, and who you are becoming. I stand for every mistake, misstep, triumph, and victory. I stand for the power that is intending to be revealed. Do not settle, not now, not ever. You are experience here to experience yourself. Get to living, get to loving, get to experiencing experience full-out!

Close Encounters of the Spiritual Human Kind

How could I have known that your gift would be my pain? How could I have seen loss as the path to healing? How could my ability to break be my wholeness? How is it you loved me so much that you would bestow such great gifts upon me?

Dearest, you led me down what appeared to be shadowed paths. I could not see. What jumped out left me afraid, what dug into me created wounds and holes in my heart, and what pierced through the dark caused me to cower inside myself. I wanted to run and hide and I did, again and again. In each age and stage there was a reason to find another place to hide, a new crevice to bury another piece of me, a new story to tell myself about who I was. But how could I have known it was all false? It all appeared so real—felt so painfully real.

Despite my choices, despite my outward intentions and affirmations, YOU kept sending the gifts. They piled on and they piled high. They became heavier and denser, more frequent and larger. There were so many that they built walls around me and the only way out was through them. Finally that one last gift arrived and the wall was too high; either they were going to cave in on top of me or I had to break through them. Either way, I now see that it was still Love being poured upon me.

How could I have known? How could I have known the whole picture? I could not see beyond what was around me surrounding me. Then I broke, maybe I broke through. They seemed to be one in the same. I turned and looked back at the block I had just moved beyond. On the outer side I saw a covering of mirrors, beautiful reflections of whom I had been, who I was, and who I was intended to be. It was in that moment that I realized true love. I let myself see magnificence. It is because within the mirror there was no longer just the brokenness, the pain, and the darkness staring back. I could not only see the wounds, insecurities, and inhibitions, but I could see Light within the eyes and hovering just off the edge of the skin. I could see the strength of perseverance, the courage of having lived through, the commitment to love, and the conviction to rise above. I could see the whole self instead of the distorted perception of a story I had let myself believe. I got too caught up in that story. I chose to close the book and be in the real, I chose to awaken to the Allness that is. Within the gifts of pain you bestowed have been secret chambers where you hid my courage, my power, my compassion, my love, and my real heart.

Dear Soul, thank YOU for giving me back to me. Thank YOU for loving me enough to not withhold anything necessary for my growth, evolution, and transformation. Thank YOU for always cherishing me enough and gifting me beyond my wildest dreams. I embrace my beautiful gifts with deep gratitude, acceptance, and love and I now realize that I have so many. But now all of my gifts are too great for me to hold any longer. I must share them, both the dark ones and the Light ones. In that I honor YOU and your love for me.

Can I tell this secret? May I let it out to one and all that they know this is their story too? Can I reveal to them their bounty? Can I let them know that gifts have been coming forth from the moment of their conception? Shall I share that their pain is their ultimate gift? Will they be able to see that your love has been golden and pure? It is the story of each one, it is the journey of the Soul, it is the path of wholeness, it is the walk back Home . . . and there's no place like Home.

26

Analyzing

Life brings many complexities. At some point or another an obstacle arises and initiates the question "Why?" When things do not make sense, it is human nature to desire understanding. Any individual in pain wants to instantly make sense of the chaos. Thoughts float through the mind in search of a purpose for the situation at hand. "I must understand why things are happening as they are. I have to make sense of it all."

Have you known that place? Have you been in a state of confusion, chaos, challenge, or pain where you questioned the meaning behind it all? Can you look back and see a moment in time where you were running here and there just so you would not have to be where you were? You were seeking a solution, an antidote, a quick fix, or a long nap, a smoke, a drink, another one-night stand, a new wardrobe, an extravagant trip, a grand spiritual experience, just something, anything to distract you from the pain. All the while, these numbing agents could not convince you that this was all part of the journey you are on. It is the dark night of the soul, the place where nothing appears to make sense, emotions are high, energy is low, and the pain never-ending. It is the place of believing that life just happens to you instead of the bold, in-your-face truth that you created it all as a means for life to happen through you.

There is one ultimate purpose of the journey, for you to experience your Self. This purpose will initiate everything necessary for you to get to the truth of who you are. However, you decided to make it colorful, filled with adventure and drama. But there has always been a safety mechanism. Love is embedded in your programming.

Love will guide every step and when you are not resonating with your Allness, Love's high frequency field will activate to uproot anything unlike itself. This creates a lot of change, often uncomfortable. The more rapidly you align with the knowing that you are the vibration of Love, the greater chance your unloved pieces have of being brought to the surface for transmutation—and peace.

The fact is, two unlike vibrations cannot exist in the same space. In addition, the higher frequency will always be the place of greater resonance, meaning lower frequencies will continue to rise toward that. How does one rise up? By going deep, either by being forced to or by choosing to do so. Resistance is futile, as the little orphaned wounded ones scream out, "I'll be back!" The unacknowledged vibrations within you will keep raising their voices until they are embraced. In that moment of embrace, those people around you that have held the same vibration will either also shift or will move out of your experience. Then, the orphans are no more.

The journey of experience experiencing itself is one of deep diving through time and space on the inner landscape. There is no other way to reach the Truth of YOU. These moments of deep excavation are so that the orphaned ones may be brought up out of the shadows and into the Light of awareness. They hold your untruths, the wounds they cling to like a worn soft blanket they cower under. Here they play out, over and over again, the beliefs, lies, and patterns that have been buried, layer upon layer, at your very core. But they are not them, they are not you. Yet they sit in your core, diminishing will and personal power.

Analyzing the outside experience is necessary only as a means to turn inward. Don't let it be more of a distraction but see, hear, and receive it as soul guidance. This means really anchoring in the perspective that the world is happening through you instead of to you. As outwardly focused beings, the world and everything that happens within it, can only serve. It is always, in all ways, pointing you at YOU. It is asking you to heal, shed, open, and allow. It is asking this again and again and again so that you can get to the microscopic truth of everything in your life. In doing so, you accept admission to view the macroscopic truth that YOU are. The world is your theater, your life the movie.

The more time you are willing to be introspective, the greater degree of healing will occur. Do not step gingerly into a healing experience. Immerse yourself so that you can experience the depths of this journey to freedom. The inner walk will allow you to engage fully in the cycle of healing, which is always the same: awareness, acceptance, and forgiveness. Let awareness be full awareness of your situation, in all of its pettiness, judgment, and rage. Go into complete acceptance bright eyed, not just peeking. Don't try to convince yourself the situation is smaller or better. You can no longer afford to avoid, justify, or deny the truth. And you will realize that knowing the truth will not kill you. That is the moment you may open the doorway to forgiveness.

Forgive yourself and forgive others. You do not have to be perfect because imperfect is good enough. It really is alright to be human. Now appreciate the incredible things you have done and who you have been. Sit in gratitude that your creation allowed you the experience of living, learning, and growing. Do not worry; you have time to clean up your messes. You will have the opportunity to hone and spread your message. You are in training as the holy messenger. Relax; you are allowed to have fun along the way. Each time you allow the cycle to turn, you open to an opportunity to redefine the experience. Every turn brings you closer to the grand realization of who YOU really are.

You are not on a journey, YOU are the journey. That journey is asking you to experience YOU in discovery. This means that there is no end goal or destination but a never-ending path of realizing ALL that you are. Step into the magnificence of infinite possibility.

Ultimately you are to discover that you are Love and you are loved. This realization will occur on ever-deepening levels as you allow recognition within everything as you. Anchoring into the feeling of being loved is your greatest access to power. In doing so, you will learn how to dance with life, regardless of the costume, face, or synchronicity that appears. There will come a point where you will not need to know, figure out, or understand. You will not need to define. There will come the moment you will know, you will figure into, you will stand in, and you will be definitive. This can happen in any moment.

27

Defining Moments

There comes a moment when you realize that where you are is not where you should be. All of a sudden the world looks different. The symbols, signs, and synchronicities move you beyond the normal everyday functioning of the average human. You are able to see how people move about unconsciously and now know you cannot ever go back to that state. The world outside, perhaps once shades of gray, now holds color. This brilliance of hues is ever increasing, revealing more and more of you in each moment.

This knowledge you have attained about yourself through conscious exploration and expansion of your being will help you move beyond constructs that hold you down, beliefs that have held you back, and experiences that no longer serve. You will begin to experience a series of defining moments that ask, "Is this what you really want? What are you willing to experience yourself as? Who can you be? How can you express? What are you really willing to have? Can you keep yourself there?"

These defining moments are when synchronicity stares you in the face and says, "Yes. Here you are in all of your glory. Dare not to step back from the magnificence you are revealing as." These moments will keep you dancing between "Can I?" and "I can!" until you anchor fully in the knowing that you are All that is. You will feel choices and decisions well up. You may view yourself in awe, wondering what has come over you. But trust. Your world will reflect what needs to happen. It will always guide you to your go(o)d. The Universe is always talking to you about YOU.

This is not from a place of arrogance or disrespect of the Almighty Presence. It is not to be blasphemous or hedonistic. It is from a place of honoring and reverence that the Divine is capable of playing however it so chooses—and it chose YOU.

One can never comprehend the depth and expansiveness of what they are until they have the courage—yes, the courage—to allow it in and through. How do you hold back? How do you hold it away? What are you too afraid to allow? What do you feel too unworthy to have touch you? I ask you now to let it in. Let yourself feel the softness of your own touch, the gentle whisper of it in your ear, the sweet scent of it wrapped around you, the rise it creates within you from core to depths you have never known and heights you had no idea existed. You need do nothing. Your presence is enough. Allow it, let it in. Just close your eyes and know it has been there all along. It is not outside of you, it is with you. It is YOU. It is ALL YOU. Do not be mistaken, it is nothing on the outside, it is something that wells up within you until it overflows constantly and consistently so that you discover that is all you are.

What I want you most to understand is that this has nothing to do with the outside. Can you be more than the personality you believe yourself to be? Can you be the experiencing of everything? Can you cherish and experience all that is around you as if you were the master artist creating it all? Cultivate this and you will find it is all that appears in your experience. How does creation well up from within you? This is the infinite expanse that exists. We all have it. It is YOU. And it is THEM, it is WE, and it is the ONE.

We are not considered powerful by the degree to which we make people see and hear us. We are not great because we tell, teach, guide, perform, do, create, or manifest in the world. Our magnificence is not dependent upon popularity, material status, or external appearance. Those whom have been great life catalysts and transformers have done so by their example as creation in the world. They feel a resonance and connection to what surrounds them.

It is by being the example that we tell, teach, guide, and lead. It is exemplifying how Love, truth, integrity, value, compassion, authenticity, and presence breathe in the world, express, experience, and engage in experiencing—as YOU.

What are you ready to experience in your life? What will you let yourself have? What will you make your possibility? What are you saying "YES" to today? Why wait, what is the point in waiting until tomorrow? Make your commitment to YES today! Start by cleaning up your thoughts. Clear up how you really feel and save yourself from the tendencies to belittle, doubt, and withhold! Most of all—NOW HEAR THIS—get rid of ALL the stories. You know the ones about why you can't, who is in your way, how you have been hurt, why you are not good enough, smart enough, free enough, ready enough, strong enough, prepared enough, rich enough, attractive enough, or any other enough. Get on with it, all of it. The world around you is showing you YOU. What is your YES today?

28

Making Meaning

Be comfortable with being human, but do not believe that it is all that you are. It is part of the experience that you have, but it is not ultimately who you are. You are the energy of the Divine, which has access to multiple universes and can use all of that as you need. At this time, you chose a learning experience as a human. However you are greater than the finite experiences of this planet. You are the planet and everything in it, you are the Universe and it's speaking to you. You are the language that is the expression between you and the greater presence of you. In order to fully know yourself, be willing to perceive this subtler level. When you do, you will see how truly vast, creative, and ingenious you are.

Each family member and friend you have chosen to be part of this experience with is also greater than you perceive them to be. They too are vast, creative, and ingenious in orchestrating the perfect storylines. Though bodies have been formed by being human, your essence is love, of love, and in love. In addition, despite the appearances, every action is with love. This love essence is your true creative power and potential. It is your divinity expressing itself.

You *experience* as human, you *create* as god, but you *are* Love. When your focus and pulsation is driven by your humanness, you will create what is needed for the current perspective. It may manifest your chaos, dysfunction, and obstacles if there are unhealed parts still guiding the human experience. It can manifest your dreams, desires, and miracles if you anchor in what is the whole of you.

At your core is your divine angelic self. It is also creating on your behalf. It acts as your fairy godmother, so to speak, by inserting the necessary symbols and signs within the human condition. These messages are there to assist you in creating meaning and connection within the experience. Meaning will guide you toward your truth, your true essence. With every breath you take, you are entering into creation. This is not intended to be a struggle to stay alive as long as you can in an expanse of time that will continue on without you. You are art of the procreation of life, in other words you are all for creating more life. By breathing out creative force, you will the unfolding of creation on a moment-by-moment basis. Through the breath you move from remembering who you are to forgetting and to remembering once again.

It is up to you to choose how to create each moment. If in a state of truth, each birthing moment will be imprinted with the love frequency. In the moments you breathe with fear, you lock within those births the DNA structure of your fear, confining that creation to the narrow bonds of illusion. In leaning back into those moments, and making love to them, you make meaning for yourself as to why they were necessary for you.

You are the hand of God that touches. You are the feet of God that moves. You are the voice of God that speaks and the mind of God that imagines. You are the body of God that connects, the soul of God that creates, and the heart of God that Loves. You are all of these consciously or unconsciously. God is unbiased in your decisions of what to create. God loves you enough to give you anything your mind and heart can hold. Will you be conscious or unconscious in your will to express? Either way the Universe celebrates your choice with a Yes!

What is the next step? The next lesson? The next sign, symbol, or synchronicity? Look around and you shall see the Universe smiling at you, speaking constantly to you, in fact. It will come through the Light and the shadow, the magical and the mundane, the ordinary and the extraordinary. Your listening and remembering will join in the celebration that is always happening.

Will you fall into forgetfulness again? Of course, that could occur. And then you will have to awaken, again, to all of who you are. The Universe will call, it will whisper, and at times it will yell. Each time you remember that an amazing dialogue is taking place, your heart will delight, your mind will become alive, and your soul will engage its re-union. You are not a guest that is joining the journey of life. You are life, happening in each and every moment, as each and every thing.

What you do in this life is extremely important. The details are really of no consequence to any other, but they are of significance to your soul. Your soul has created the Universe and all of its dialogue for you to know the truth of who you are, the truth of you as the essence of Love. You have been making meaning all along through every symbol, sign, message, and synchronicity. You have done so because, at your core, you know your good intent. You know your Oneness and interconnectedness. You are only creating a full symphony of expression to bring this melody of Love out in the most beautiful song that may be sung. You have orchestrated every instrument and note of the Universe to be in concert with you. How simply magnificent you are. Is the Universe talking to you? Well, of course. To you, through you, in you, and as you. You are the YOU-niverse. YOU are the Uni-verse—One verse!

Review of Language Play: Creative Capacity

Language Play is not work. It is play, intended to be engaged in with curiosity and adventure. Allow yourself to have an ongoing conversation with the Universe.

Language Play Creative Capacity is where the field of infinite possibility begins. Your interaction in a conscious way, through the use of your creative capacity, can provide the true experience spirit essence having a completely spiritual experience . . . Play-fully bringing into form the creation that is you.

The Story

- What is the story I have hung onto?
- What are the emotions I have held?
- Where on the Rainbow Bridge am I?
- Where is the oneness of emotions?
- Where am I in the oneness of all things?

Analysis

- Write out your Godburst creation. Incorporate all the elements of your life that were the Essence of Divine, fragmented, to show you YOU.
- What did you ask to learn?
- What gifts did you arrive with?
- What destiny did you desire to unfold?

Meaning

- What things have brought true meaning to my life?
- What signs appear which help me tap into that meaning?
- What signs and symbols have best expressed as a language for me?

Additional Resources

Animal Symbolism

Animal-Speak: The Spiritual and Magical Powers of Animals Great & Small by Ted Andrews

Nature-Speak: Signs, Omens, and Messages in Nature by Ted Andrews

What the Walrus Knows by Sarah Seidelmann

Body Symbolism

The Secret Language of the Body: The Essential Guide to Health and Wellness by Inna Segal

You Can Heal Your Life by Louise Hay

Car Symbolism

My Car My Self by Ken Kizer, Center for Awareness

Dream Symbolism

The Magical, Mystical, Marvelous World of Dreams by Wilda B. Tanner

Name Symbolism

Know the Name; Know the Person: How a Name Can Predict Thoughts, Feelings, and Actions by Sharon Lynn Wyeth

Number Symbolism

Angel Numbers 101: The Meaning of Numbers 111, 123, 444, and Other Number Sequences by Doreen Virtue

The Numerology Kit by Carol Adrienne

The Complete Book of Numerology by David A. Phillips

Acknowledgments

I hold sincere love and gratitude for every person, symbol, sign, and synchronicity that has crossed my path, named and unnamed, because these were clues, messages, angels, teachers, and guides for me. I am a composite of all those who have touched me and every experience integrated. They have brought me to a deeper sense of awe, wonder, and Oneness.

Special appreciation and deep love to those whom have touched my life in a profound way: Inna Segal, Maureen Moss, Aleya Dao, Dr. Sue Morter, Iyanla Vanzant, Almasi Wilcots, Ken and Renee Kizer, Calvin Styles, Amy Zerner, Monte Farber, Tuck Self, Virginia Way, Christina Sullivan, Sheila Ruff, and Laura Tallman.

From the bottom of my heart and soul, I want to extend special appreciation to William Gladstone, Kenichi Sugihara, Nancy Sugihara, and Kenzi Sugihara. Thank you for your guidance and believing in my voice. Deep gratitude and appreciation to Brandy Jackson, Jeff Gerstl, the Voice America Network, Cynthia Torp, and Puja Network for such wonderful platforms to share my voice.

My deep unconditional love to you, Dr. Ajit and Raj Randhawa, Mitti, Gogi, and Nikki. Charan Randhawa, especially deep gratitude to you and msndrstddesigns.com for creating my websites, helping me navigate technology, and being an intuitive artistic genius. You have been an angel in my life's work. Rick Singh, you have been an incredible teacher for me in this life. Sage and Krish, there are no brighter lights in my experience, you are amazing representations of the Divine.

Always… in all ways,
In Love, of Love, with Love and Laughter,
Simran

About the Author

Speaker – Catalyst – Visionary – Humorist – Rebel

Simran Singh—a creative visionary, transformational catalyst, and humorist in the realms of metaphysics, spirituality, and motivation—is the award winning publisher of *11:11 Magazine*. She hosts the #1-rated, syndicated *11:11 Talk Radio on VoiceAmerica 7th Wave* and *On the Lighter Side Radio* broadcast on *World Puja Network*.

Her 11:11 Media Resources, launched in 2008, are freely gifted to enhance conscious evolution and empowered living.

Globally reaching hundreds of thousands of individuals with her impassioned wisdom, Simran is well known to assist people in understanding the conversation the Universe is having with every individual. Leading change agents, best-selling authors, world-renowned healers, and motivational speakers endorse Simran's work as a unique source of powerful truth, wisdom, and rich content. Her philosophy of "being an example of authenticity and compassion, and of bold experience and creation," catalyzes profound change.

As author of *Conversations with the Universe*, Simran walks her talk by letting all go in order to live boldly during the experience of a "one-year, one woman live-streamed RV-tour around the country." *The Rebel Road is to be* live-streamed on One World Puja Network and is her vision of freeing people from their self-imposed limitations to live life fearlessly, boldly, and in the full, passionate adventure of the heart's desire to awaken the infinite possibility and creative flow that is our natural inheritance.

Simran Singh's Websites

Simran Singh	www.Simran-Singh.com
The Rebel Road – Connect the Dots	www.TheRebelRoad.com
11:11 Magazine FREE Soul Curriculum	www.1111mag.com
11:11 Talk Radio - Voice America	www.voiceamerica.com/Show/1536
11:11 Innerviews on The Lighter Side One World Puja Network	www.worldpuja.org/innerviews.php

Connect with Simran Singh

Facebook	Simran	www.facebook.com/SimranSingh1111
	11:11	www.facebook.com/1111Magazine
Twitter	Simran	http://twitter.com/simransingh1111
	11:11	http://twitter.com/1111magazine
LinkedIn		http://www.linkedin.com/in/simransingh1111
YouTube		http://www.youtube.com/simransingh1111

Simran Singh Inspirations

Blogs	http://simransingh1111.wordpress.com
Pinterest	http://pinterest.com/simransingh1111/